Henry Swinburne

Supplement to Mr. Swinburne's Travels through Spain

Being a Journey from Bayonne to Marseilles

Henry Swinburne

Supplement to Mr. Swinburne's Travels through Spain
Being a Journey from Bayonne to Marseilles

ISBN/EAN: 9783744756440

Printed in Europe, USA, Canada, Australia, Japan

Cover: Foto ©Andreas Hilbeck / pixelio.de

More available books at **www.hansebooks.com**

S.^t......   W.^m....... sculp: Impensis ....

HENRY SWINBURNE ESQ.^R

SUPPLEMENT

TO

Mr. SWINBURNE's

TRAVELS THROUGH SPAIN.

BEING A

JOURNEY

FROM

BAYONNE

TO

MARSEILLES.

LONDON:

PRINTED BY J. DAVIS,

FOR P. ELMSLY, IN THE STRAND.

M.DCC.LXXXVII.

INTRODUCTION.

THE following pages might have ferved as a prelude to my Neapolitan tour, but at the time of its appearance, I was extremely unwilling to undertake a defcription of any part of France, and therefore, inftead of continuing the account of my Travels from the confines of Spain, I chofe to commence my narrative, at the inftant of our leaving Marfeilles. France is a kingdom fo often vifited by Englifh travellers, that I had little hopes of collecting new materials either for entertainment or inftruction; but I am fince become confcious that this omiffion deftroys the connection between my Letters on Spain and my Travels in Italy, and hurries my reader too abruptly from the Ocean to the Mediterranean fea. To fupply this deficiency, I now publifh my obfervations on the intervening provinces, and hope they will fill up the chafm in a fatisfactory manner, and thus form one regular and well-connected feries of travels.

J O U R N E Y

F R O M

B A Y O N N E

T O

M A R S E I L L E S.

———————◆———————

L E T T E R I.

Tarbes, June 22, 1776.

AFTER completing a circle of sixteen hundred miles, I am at length returned to the point from which I took my departure in October. My laft letter informed you briefly, that I had paffed the limits of the Spanifh dominions, and was once more landed on the territories of France. Thefe monarchies are divided by the waters of the Bidaffoa, impetuous and difficult at high tide, but at other times, clear and placid, flowing through a delicious vale, that ill accords with the ideas generally entertained of the boundaries between two mighty empires: the eafe with which we were ferried over, and the abfence of all military parade, rendered it ftill more unlike; but no fooner did we fet foot on French ground, than we were made fenfible of the feparation; a moft rigorous fearch of our baggage took place; the ferenity of the weather was a fortunate circumftance, for every article belonging to us was taken out of the trunks, and fpread upon the grafs; the collecting and ftowing of them again in their refpective places, confumed the beft part of the day, and night overtook us before we could reach Saint Jean de Luz.* The fituation of this town is charming. The Ninette falls into the fea at

---

* Luz, or Luis, fignifies mud in Bafque, very characteriftic of the foil.

a fmall

a small distance below, having first swelled out into a double bay, capable of admitting vessels of considerable tonnage; but its entrance is difficult, and the road dangerous in stormy weather. The shore is lined with buildings, and sheltered by hills of moderate elevation, which rise gently all around, contracting their green slopes and woody summits with this grand expanse of water. The adjacent country is highly and variously cultivated, and the Pyrenean mountains, which display softer features than eminences of similar height usually possess, close in the back ground with pleasing dignity.

The language peculiar to the province of Labour * is Basque, which, I am informed, bears little affinity to any of the neighbouring dialects, and claims a lineal descent from the aboriginal tongue of the Cantabrians. I fear no monuments remain to guide etymologists in a research how far this claim is admissible, or how much the language is altered, improved, or degenerated from the old stock : it abounds in vowels, and its sounds are soft and musical.

The spirit of their ancestors still lives in the Basques and their neighbours the Biscayners, who boast of the same origin : all we read in ancient history of the agility, perseverance, and industry, of the Cantabrians, may be recognized at this day in every part of these provinces. Their early habits of exercise improve the neatness of limb and flexibility of muscles which distinguish them when adults : if they dance to the sound of their native tambourine, the fire of their character pervades and animates the whole frame. Ancient Greece herself could not present her painters and sculptors with models of more exquisite elegance than the young women of this country ; a flowing white veil fastened with bunches of red ribbons, and the freedom which their short garments leave for every movement, enhance the natural beauty of their form.

From Saint Jean to Bayonne the landscape is delightful, the soil rich in productions of many kinds, the surface pleasantly uneven and crowned with noble woods, but the roads from the banks of the Bidassoa are insufferably bad. I cannot account for this uncommon neglect either on political or œconomical principles, especially as the highways in the next Spanish province, are judiciously made, and carefully maintained. Can it proceed from the inveteracy of ancient habits, which perpetuates the nuisance, and prevents the present set of ministers from thinking themselves authorized to facilitate

* A corruption of *Lapurdum*, the ancient name of Bayonne.

a commua communication, which their predeceffors had wifely rendered as difficult as poffible? Our carriages, which had paffed unbroken over the rocks of Valencia, and through the clays of Andalufia, were fhattered to pieces during this fhort journey.

* Bayonne is fituated three miles from the Bay of Bifcay, at the conflux of the rivers Adorer and Nive, both navigable; but their mouth is embarraffed with fhifting fands, which it requires the fkill of an experienced pilot to avoid. The hills on each fide are defended by fortifications, traced after the plans of Marfhal Vauban, in order to render impregnable a place that was long the Key of France, and as fuch frequently but unfuccefsfully attempted by the Spaniards: although every apprehenfion from that quarter has ceafed fince the crown of Spain has been fixed on the brow of a prince of the Bourbon line, the works are neverthelefs kept up, and a confiderable garrifon maintained to man them. Twenty-fix thoufand inhabitants are computed to refide in Bayonne, near four thoufand of which are of the Jewifh perfuafion: when this perfecuted race of men was driven out of Spain and Portugal, great numbers of them took refuge here; they increafed fo rapidly, as foon to feel the neceffity of fending forth a colony to Bordeaux, where it has flourifhed furprifingly by brokerage and privateering.

Bayonne was an independant vifcounty till fubdued by the kings of England, dukes of Aquitaine: in 1450, when they were ftripped of all their continental poffeffions, it paffed with the reft under the dominion of Charles the Seventh, king of France. Commerce is here carried on with great fpirit; the neighbouring provinces of France draw a large proportion of their foreign commodities from this port, and fend hither in return their fuperfluous productions to be forwarded to a proper market; but the moft lucrative branches of its traffic are fupported by an intercourfe with Spain. A great number of fhips are built here, as many materials for conftruction are to be had at the firft hand. In war-time Bayonne fits out ftout and well-appointed privateers, and in days of peace its mariners approve themfelves hardy and induftrious in commercial purfuits; they were the firft that attempted the whale and Newfoundland fifheries, and invented the method of curing cod; they difcovered Canada, and penetrated into the heart of

* Bayonne fignifies in Bafque a *good Bay.*

that

that vaft and favage region, by failing up the river of Saint Laurence, thus opening a new feene for the ambition and animofity of two rival nations.

The coachmaker having pronounced our chaifes incapable of proceeding, without great repairs, we rode poft to Tarbes : the hafte we made to reach this city, and the intenfe heat of the day, precluded all obfervations on the places we pafled through.

LETTER II.

Tarbes, June 29.

TARBES, the capital of the province of Bigorre, is an open city widely fpread in the center of a large plain : it has more the appearance of a great village than of an epifcopal fee. The waters of the Adour, which are conducted through it in various channels, procure fignal conveniencies to the inhabitants, but render the air damp and chilly.

The cathedral is very ancient, and fuppofed to occupy the fite of *Begora*, or *Caftrum Begorrenfe*, whence the country derives its name; its bifhop fat among the prelates of the council held at Agde in 506. The ruins of a caftle fill part of the central divifion of the town, to which the other quarters were originally fuburbs.

The general affembly of the ftates of Bigorre meets annually at Tarbes, whofe prelate is their perpetual prefident; the other members are feven abbots or priors, two commanders of the order of Maltha, twelve barons, and twenty-eight deputies of towns*. Each branch of adminiftration has its vote, and two out of the three fuffice to carry a point. In thefe affemblies all public bufinefs is difcuffed, and all affeffments made. In countries that enjoy the privilege of meeting annually, taxation and expenditure are generally managed in a manner lefs onerous to the fubject, than in thofe provinces, which, having been long the peculiar domain of the French monarch, or

---

* This is the account I received in the country. The geographical defcriptions of Bigorre compofe the ftates of one bifhop, four abbots, one commander, twelve barons, fome gentlemen, and the deputies of the townfhips.

acquired

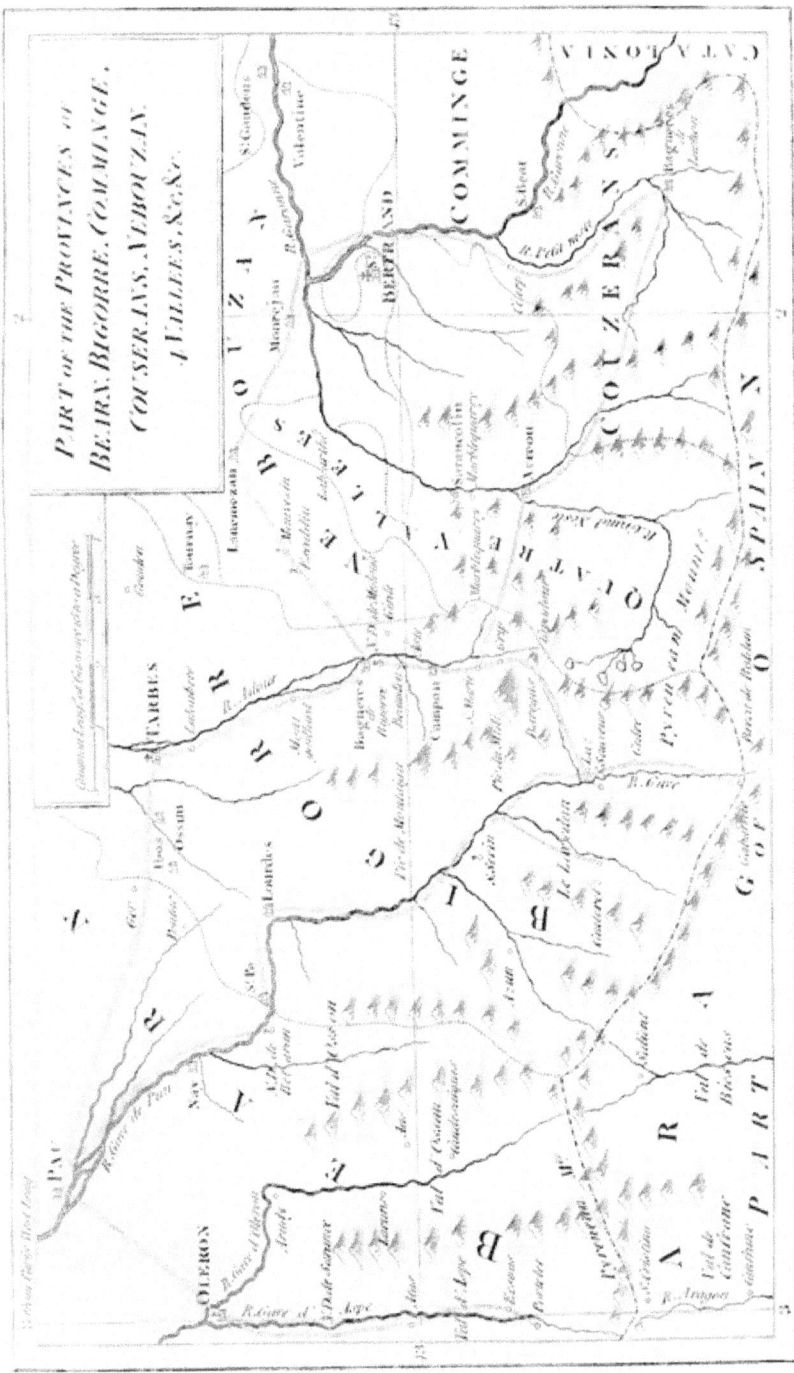

PART OF THE PROVINCES OF
BEARN, BIGORRE, COMMINGE,
COUSERANS, NEBOUZAN,
VALLIES, &c. &c.

acquired by conqueſt, retain no traces of liberty, and are abandoned to the merciless rule of financiers.

The little freedom ſtill apparent in Bigorre is the ghoſt of that conſtitution, which the ancient inhabitants maintained in full force againſt the eſſorts of ſeveral races of ſovereigns, all of whom felt a deſire of ſubverting it, but either failed in the attempt, or foreſaw that their ſafety depended upon their compliance with the eſtabliſhed regulations. The Bigorri were a people of Gaul, claſſed by the Romans among the nations of the third Aquitania. In the ninth century, a particular count or governor was firſt ſent to preſide over them, and in the common courſe of events, the power of theſe counts became hereditary. Towards the cloſe of the fourteenth century, this province was united to the viſcounty of Bearn; it afterwards formed a part of the dominions of Navarre, and with that kingdom fell to the crown of France, by the acceſſion of Henry the Fourth.

The people of Bigorre have a warm attachment to the place of their birth, and ſeldom fail to return to it with the money they have earned in various parts of the kingdom, in order to purchaſe a little land, and wind off the remnants of the clew of life, among the companions of their youth. Cookery is a favourite profeſſion of theirs, but in every trade they become conſpicuous by their induſtry. They are far from a comely race, and when advanced in years are troubled with wens on the throat; their ſtature is rather below what the Engliſh eſteem the middle ſize; but they are muſcular and active, and dance with uncommon ſpirit and preciſion. In ſummer they go barefoot, though the ſoil is full of ſtones, and only put on ſlippers when about to dance. Their clothes are always neat and in good condition, their circumſtances being much eaſier than thoſe of the French peaſantry in other provinces; the women wear a red hood, that fits the head like a nun's veil, and falls down to the waiſt. In the diſtrict of Oſſun the men ſtill adhere to the mode of dreſs that prevailed in the reign of Henry the Fourth, and probably in times of much greater antiquity; a ſmall round bonnet, a brown jacket and doublet laced down the ſeams with white, red cuffs, and trunk-hoſe, diſtinguiſh them from all their neighbours; they are principally employed as carriers, and have long enjoyed the reputation of unſullied honeſty.

The provincial dialect of Bigorre is extremely uncouth to the ear of a ſtranger. Though I believe the wealthier inhabitants of Bigorre are neither

B   poſſeſſed poffeffed of more probity, nor lead more irreproachable lives than thofe of the northern parts of France, there appears to exift a greater fund of honour and honefty among the inferior ranks, at leaft as far as concerns pecuniary tranfactions among themfelves: feveral cuftoms and traits that have come to my knowledge confirm this opinion, one of which I fhall quote for its fingularity. When a peafant A, the owner of a few fheep or cows, is diftreffed for ready money, either to complete a purchafe of land, or for the immediate fuftenance of his family, he applies to fome richer neighbour B, and offers to fell him his ftock *en gazaille.* If the propofal be accepted, the property is valued and the price paid down; but notwithftanding this transfer, the feller A retains poffeffion, and pays B, by way of intereft, half the profits upon the wool and young produced; the milk remains the perquifite of A. The buyer may at any time claim and drive away his cattle, which however A has in his option to repurchafe; if he decline this offer, an eftimate is made, and whatever the property may have gained is equally fhared between them, as the lofs, if any, falls equally upon both parties. If the *gazaille* die by any common diforder, is devoured by wild beafts, or dafhed to pieces by a fall into a precipice, A makes good the damage; but an epidemical diftemper affects the interefts of B exclufively. Touching in the hand conftitutes the whole ceremony of the agreement, and fuch bargains are inviolably adhered to.

L E T T E R   III.

Bagneres de Bigorre, July 28.

WE removed from Tarbes to drink the mineral waters, and fpend the hot months among thefe mountains. The road hither is excellent, and paffes through a rapid fucceffion of grand, romantic, and pleafing profpects, where the uncommon richnefs of the foil is ably feconded by the intelligent induftry of the cultivators. Near Tarbes the plain is fo extenfive, that the range of hills on each fide fcarce engage the attention; a large portion of its flat furface is covered with pollard cherry trees, ferving as props to the vines, while Turkey wheat occupies the ground below. Not a fpot of land is fuffered

to

to lie in unprofitable idlenefs, except where the Adour has defolated the plains with its irrefiftible torrents that rufh down from the mountains on the melting of the fnows. We gradually drew near the entrance of a valley, the hills, as it were, approached towards us, and each lofty fummit became more diftinctly marked ; the way foon grew lefs level, and the face of the country was hidden by woods of tall oak ; in the midft of thefe groves are numerous villages, delicious habitations in fummer, for every cottage is fhaded by a clump of trees, and every garden is refrefhed by copious ftreams of limpid water ; the ground rifes gently towards hills neatly cultivated, and ftrewed with a beautiful variety of productions. At length the vale narrows to a point like the bottom of a net, and is intirely clofed up by the buildings of Bagneres ; an awful pile of mountains rudely thrown together, preffes behind upon the green woody heights that overhang the town : the low lands before it are covered with crops of divers forts of grain, but chiefly abound in Turkey wheat: the method of managing it is to raife the feed in garden beds, then plant out the fhoots in the fields, towards the end of May, in rows two feet diftant from each other; as foon as they have acquired ftrength fufficient, and the flowers appear, kidney beans are fet at the foot of each plant ; hence forward it ferves as a pole for the bean, which is gathered before the maize is fit to remove. In September, the fruit-bearing part of the plant being impregnated, the ftalk that produced the pollen is cut away, and with all the leaves ufed as fodder for cattle ; the remainder is left till October, a bare ftalk to ripen its feed. Millet is fown on the plots that have already yielded flax or early corn ; it ripens in October, when the fecond crop of flax begins to appear above ground. Corn is reaped with fickles or fcythes, and then fpread very thin over the field ; in a few days it is carried home in carts, if a road can be made, or in crates on the heads of the women ; then as many hands as can be procured, are employed in threfhing it out upon earthen floors, with light flails. In thefe vallies the hufbandman tears out his ftubbles by means of a triangular harrow armed with ftrong iron teeth turned forwards ; a thick oaken faplin bowed double ferves him to prefs down the harrow, and to lift it up occafionally, to fhake off the clods ; two oxen draw this machine, under the guidance of a girl, who walks on finging and knitting. This procefs drags away the weeds in this light foil, and prepares the ground for the plough. The operation of ploughing is performed very tenderly, for there is but a fcanty

B 2 covering

covering of good earth above a fhivery ftratum; two oxen, cows, horfes, and, not unfrequently, affes, are yoked together by means of a wooden bar, which keeps them at fuch a diftance afunder, that they cannot trample on the rows of plants between which they move.

All the meadows, even on the declivities of the mountains, are watered by fmall cuts from the fprings or rivers, and produce annually two crops of hay, the firft extremely abundant : the fields in the plain admit of a third mowing in October.

Bagneres contains about three thoufand inhabitants; they fubfift comfortably upon their paternal inheritances and the money they amafs from the annual vifits of ftrangers who refort hither to drink or bathe in its waters. It is furrounded with old walls, and is tolerably built, but the ftreets are narrow and crooked; the quantity of water that runs through them renders the town cool and pleafant in fummer, but in winter it is exceedingly cold on account of the vicinity of the mountains, and the heavy falls of fnow, that remain feveral months upon the ground. It has no buildings of any note. The Adour is here a fierce torrent; its waters are white like thofe of all mountain ftreams proceeding from fnows; they are diverted at feveral places from their natural courfe, and conveyed in channels acrofs the plain, and through the town, where they are employed in numberlefs ufeful operations.

Bagneres derives its name from the mineral baths, which were known and frequented by the ancient Romans, as many infcriptions and monuments ftill exifting on the fpot, fatisfactorily demonftrate; the moft explicit is to be feen in the fquare, dedicated to the nymphs of thefe falutiferous waters.

NYMPHISPROSALVTESVASEVERSERANVSVSLM.

The peafants of the neighbourhood are a lively race, and often affemble in a fhady walk near the gates to dance. One of the Queens of Navarre remitted all fines upon alienation of property at Bagneres, on condition that a fmall fum fhould be levied upon each perfon admitted to his freedom, and fpent in bonefires and other merry expences at Midfummer.

The fituation of this place is happily calculated for all exercifes that tend to the recovery of health; it is built in a flat and upon a very dry foil; every part of it enjoys an eafy communication with the fields, the banks of the river, or the high roads, where the weaker fort of vifitants may breathe

the frefh air, and regain ftrength by moderate exertions ; while the more vigorous, who repair to Bagneres for the fake of amufement, may climb delightful
hills, and wander among fhady groves through a never-ending variety of
landfcape.　The plain and eminences are traverfed by innumerable paths
acceffible to horfemen as well as foot-paffengers ; the high grounds are not like
thofe in the Alps, broken and precipitous, but eafily floped, and clothed
with foft and pleafant verdure.　The timber that crowns their fummits is of
the nobleft fize.　In the heart of cultivation, and near the foot of the mountains, the Spanifh cheftnut predominates intermingled with cherry, walnut, and
other fruit trees, round which the vine entwines its tendrils.　Higher up the
extent of pafture becomes more confiderable ; the middle regions of the mountains are darkened with woods of beech overhung by forefts of filver fir, and
above all, black pinnacles of rocks fhoot up to a frightful height, with here
and there a wreath of fnow preferved unmelted through the fummer by the
protection of their fhade.　That fide of the mountains which faces the noon
tide fun is richly covered with wood, but the oppofite flope is feldom fo beautiful, for it produces fewer trees and thofe of a ftunted growth ; the greateft
part of thefe forefts is the common property of the neighbouring villages, and
as high as carriage can be eafily contrived, is cut after a regular but carelefs
manner, for the fupply of fuel, and the purpofes of hufbandry.

L E T T E R IV.

I HAVE referved the principal merit of Bagneres for the laft part of my
defcription, and fhall devote this letter to its medicinal waters ; they alone
have refcued this valley from the obfcurity which involves fo many neighbouring beautiful diftricts ; a great number of boiling, lukewarm, and cold
ftreams, iffue out of the fides of the mountain that covers the town on the
weftern afpect ; all of them poffefs, or are fuppofed to poffefs, very ftrong
healing qualities, which each patient applies with great confidence to his
particular diforder, under the directions of the phyficians of the place.
The fummit of this mountain is indented with a large hollow, fimilar to the

crater

crater of a volcano, and I have no doubt but fire has been emitted from this cup at some period beyond the reach of hiftory; the fire which was then fufficient to produce explofions, and to caft forth torrents of lava, ftill retains the power, in its weaker ftate, of imparting virtue in various degrees to the mineral fprings that flow from the mountain where its focus is eftablifhed. *

The number of wells and baths amounts to thirty; fome are covered in for the ufe of patients that can afford to pay for their cures. Others are open pools, where the poorer clafs gargle their ulcerous throats, or lave their fores, gratis. The heat of fome fpouts is at firft almoft infupportable, but gradually grows lefs painful. I have feen people expofe their difeafed limbs to the boiling ftream for more than a quarter of an hour at a time. The hotteft fpring raifes the quickfilver in Fahrenheit's thermometer to 123 degrees, while the cooleft caufes it to afcend no higher than 86. Out of the thirty different fources, two are exactly equal in heat to that of the human body, ten below, and eighteen above it. Their medicinal qualities differ no lefs effentially than their degrees of heat; for the waters of the Queen's bath are ftrongly purgative, thofe of Salut and Le Pré diuretic and cooling. The bath of Salut is fituated about a mile from the town, among the mountains; a pleafant winding road leads to it, through beautiful fields planted with clumps of cheftnut trees. The houfes and groves on the furrounding hills cheer the profpect; but in fo hot a feafon, and in this latitude, an avenue would be a great improvement and relief to the patients. The fpring is copious and equal to the demands of the crowds that flock round it on holidays, when every perfon may drink his fill for the value of three farthings Englifh: the vogue is fo great, that two guineas have been taken in one morning, at this low price. From the drinking place the waters are conveyed into two marble troughs, which are in conftant ufe during the whole feafon. Seniority of refidence conftitutes the right of bathing, and therefore many late comers, who forefee but a diftant profpect of being

* When I vifited the Pyrenees, I had little acquaintance with volcanoes, their diftinctive features and productions, therefore I can bring no proofs, but analogy, of their priftine exiftence near Bagneres; the circular lakes on the mountains, the hot, fulphureous vapours and waters, the caverns, bafons, and forms of the ground, are the tokens, which, being impreffed on my memory, convince me that volcanoes have in remote ages difturbed the face of that country. The knowledge requifite for difcovering volcano traces in rocks, foils, and minerals, is almoft unattainable without a vifit to thofe regions where nature is actually employed in thofe tremendous operations.

accommodated

accommodated with an hour of Salut, take up with the other baths of inferior reputation, but perhaps equal efficacy. The degree of heat of Salut is 88! ; when evaporated by a flow equal fire, the furface of its water is covered with a pellicle formed by fmall infipid chryftals, which towards the completion of the evaporation acquire confiderable acritude. Thefe waters contain no particles of iron, but fmall parallelopiped pyrites are frequently found in them, of a bright golden colour, and about an inch long.

L E T T E R   V.

Bagneres, Aug. 15.

I Returned yefterday from a journey on horfeback, through the moft romantic and curious part of the Pyrenees, and haften to impart my obfervations, while each idea is ftill impreffed with force on *the tablet of my memory.*

I fet out on the fixth with fome friends, and travelled up the valley; the low grounds are finely cultivated; numberlefs ftreams pour acrofs the road, and hurry to blend their waters with thofe of the Adour, which is here confined to a narrow bed; beyond it eaftward, the mountains are covered with beautiful verdure; at their foot ftands Afté, a village belonging to the family of Grammont. *

A peafant, who refides here, earns a livelihood by fupplying the apothecaries with medicinal plants, which he gathers on the adjacent mountains, particularly that of Lieris, juftly celebrated for the immenfe and variegated fhew of flowers, that cover its elevated paftures, before fheep and cattle are let in to graze. The convent of capuchins, at Medous, oppofite Afté, is placed fo clofely under a mountain, that in winter it enjoys but two hours funfhine in the whole day; its garden is remarkable for a large volume of water, that

* In 1530 the Lord of the valley of Aure acquired the vifcounty of Afté by marriage, and his fon married the heirefs of Grammont, a family that bore a diftinguifhed part in the troubles of Navarre, in the 15th century. Their defcendants affumed the name and arms of Grammont.

iffues

iffues out of the rocks; trouts are often feen fwimming down the ftream, but if difturbed, they retire into the bowels of the mountain, to fome fubterraneous lake. The populoufnefs of this vale is fcarce credible: in the extent of three miles I reckoned near five hundred houfes, or barns. The burgh of Campan gives name to the upper diftrict, and is famous for the excellency of its butter; it acknowledges no lord but the king, and has confiderable woods and cultivated lands, appertaining to its community.

At a fmall diftance above the town, we were conducted to a celebrated grotto, in the fide of a bare mountain: the entrance is narrow and floping, but at the depth of ten feet the floor of the cavern lies nearly on a level: the vault feldom exceeds nine feet in height; its length is an hundred and four yards; the path wet and rugged; the walls and roof incruftated with chryftalizations; but all that were curious for fize, fhape, or beauty of colour, had been broken off and carried way by preceding travellers. At the end of the grotto we found a marble flab, fixed up by order of the countefs of Brionne, to commemorate, that after infinite labour, fhe, with her family and fervants, whofe names are all configned to immortality on this fubterraneous monument, penetrated thus far into the bowels of the earth, in the year 1766.

Above Campan the valley grew more confined, the hills on the right hand ftudded with trees and barns, and covered with lively verdure; thofe on the left were rocky, barren, and favage. At the chapel of Saint Mary, two branches of the Adour flow from different glens, and join their waters; we rode up the more weftern ftream to Grip, where all level ground terminates. Noble groves of fir overhang the river, which dafhes fucceffively down three romantic falls. Having taken fome refrefhment, we proceeded up the mountain by a winding, fteep, and rugged path, through a foreft of filver and fpruce firs; we occafionally caught views of the river foaming among the rocks and trees, and in one fpot darting over a vaft precipice in a full, magnificent fheet.

Upon leaving the woods we croffed a large naked plain, at the foot of the Pic du midi, the higheft mountain of the Pyrenees.* The Adour iffues out of a pyramidical hill, a few miles farther up, and winds in a fmall ftream through the rufhy paftures. Abundance of flowers animate the face of this otherwife dull fcene of nature. We were now arrived at the higheft point of land

* The Canigout in Rouffillon is nearly as high above the fea.

we

BAREGES.

we had to furmount, when we were furprifed by a very heavy fall of fnow,
that whitened all the furrounding eminences, but foon melted into rain,
and wetted us thoroughly. When the ftorm abated, and the atmofphere grew
clear, a horrible view opened down the valley of Bareges : rude and barren
mountains fhade it on both fides, and the Bafton, a foaming torrent, fills
the intermediate hollow. We defcended by the edge of the river, and entered
one of the bleakeft and moft defolate places in nature ; where not a tree
was to be feen, but the heights were feamed with yawning crevices, and
the paffages blocked up with quarries of ftone, tumbled from the cliffs by the
irrefiftible force of the waters. In this frightful chafm ftands the village of
Bareges, confifting of a fingle ftreet built along the fouth fide of the torrent.
The fituation is fo dangerous and horrid, that the inhabitants dare not abide
here in winter ; they remove all their furniture, even doors and windows,
to fuch houfes as are fuppofed moft out of the way of mifchief : a few invalid foldiers alone remain, to preferve the fprings from being buried under
the earth that flides down from the mountains. Sometimes a large volume
of water burfts out of its fide, the overplus of a lake on the fummit, and
fweeps off all before it : each year fome houfes are wafhed away by the floods,
or crufhed under the weight of fnow. The *avelanches*, or heaps of fnow that
are detached from the mountains, are often fo prodigious as to fill up the
whole bottom of the glen ; and the river has been known to roll for feveral
weeks through an arch of its own forming under this immeafureable mafs.

The mineral waters, for which Bareges is famed, iffue out of the hill in the
center of the village, and are diftributed into three baths. They are very
fetid, but clear in the glafs ; their degrees of heat rife from 89 to 112½.
They are greafy to the touch, tinge filver black, and are efteemed fovereign in
the cure of ulcers, wounds, and fcrophulous humours. The baths belong to
the king, and are entirely under the direction of his furgeons. The poor
have the ufe of a large bath covered with boards, and are fed by a tax of
fix livres impofed upon all new comers ; with this fund a comfortable dinner
is provided for them, and diftributed in prefence of the governor, a worthy
veteran, who folicited this command from a motive of gratitude, having been
cured of a dangerous wound by bathing it with thefe waters. No company
reforts hither merely for amufement ; diforders only, and thofe fevere and
inveterate ones, can induce people to inhabit thefe wild regions. There is an

C

affembly

affembly room and regular bath, when it is I know not whether a melancholy or a ludicrous fight, to behold feveral couples dancing together, fome with a leg bound up, others with an arm in a fling, and all with a feeble body and a fickly afpect.

On the 8th we continued our journey by an excellent road with a rapid defcent.—The landfcape grew gayer every ftep; trees, villages, and cultivation gradually ftole upon us as we travelled down the valley; it terminates in a fmall beautiful plain, in the front of which the ruined caftle of Saint Maria on a rocky brow prefents a groupe of objects, fuch as Salvator Rofa delighted in delineating ; mountains of ftupendous altitude environ it, and feem to pro-hibit all communication with the reft of the world ; many hamlets appear at once, half hidden by rich groves, fome rifing in the plain, others placed high up the mountains. We paffed through Luz, a confiderable town, and croffing the river Gave, into which the Bafton empties itfelf, alighted at the baths of Saint Sauveur, a moft romantic fpot. Six large houfes built on a rock overfhaded with woods, contain the company. The Gave winds under the cliff, the mountain rifes immediately behind, and on every fide cafcades are feen and heard dafhing from precipice to precipice. The waters of thefe baths are not fo hot as thofe of Bareges, but their tafte is ftill more naufeous : great quantities of faponaceous fcum are gathered in the cifterns and fpouts. There is a fpecies of harmlefs ferpent that delights in thefe waters, and fre-quently pays very unwelcome vifits to the bathers.

L E T T E R   VI.

Bagneres, Auguft 21.

AS my laft letter had long detained you among wild, mountainous fcenes, a fhort paufe was neceffary to relieve your imagination, which might in fome degree be fympathetically affected with the bodily fatigue we un-derwent in vifiting them. I have therefore fuffered a few days to elapfe before I gave you the continuation of my rambles, that you might have leifure to familiarize yourfelf with this grand ftyle of landfcape : here nature exhibits her boldeft features ; here every object is extended upon a vaft

fcale,

fcale, and the whole affemblage impreffes the fpectator with awe as well as admiration. What is left to defcribe ftill exceeds the majefty of the views which have been the fubject of my laft letters: I wifh it were poffible for me to communicate, by means of words or paintings, the rapturous fenfations excited in my mind by the fight of thofe fublime works of the Creator.

We left Saint Sauveur by funrife, repaffed the bridge of Luz, and ftruck into a road that leads up the river. As we advanced we found ourfelves immured in a narrow valley, with the Gave roaring below us, between walls of immenfe rocks, and frequently hidden from our view by thick groves of lime and oak trees. The path was wide enough for our mountain horfes, but very alarming to fome unexperienced travellers in our company; on one hand a perpendicular rock, without any parapet, laid open the deep gloomy bed of the river almoft under our feet, and a fhivery mountain preffed fo clofe upon us on the other, as to leave no room for a retreat The turns in the road, where torrents have heaped ftones, and choaked the pafs with rubbifh, are particularly diftreffing; but our horfes were fo unconcerned, and furefooted, that they foon infpired their riders with equal indifference for the furrounding perils.

The whole valley is occupied by the river and the road, with vaft piles of mountains rifing on each fide, and almoft clofing together; now and then level fpots occur at the angles of the river. We croffed a bridge romantically clothed with ivy, which hid the tremendous chafm from our eyes: huge rocks rear up their perpendicular points, and torrents rufh over them on all fides. The mountain afh, and fervice tree, blufhing with cluftered berries, bend over the precipices, and foften the harfhnefs of the wild profpect. After this the valley rather fwells out, and more room is allowed for the indefatigable induftry of the inhabitants to exert itfelf; but great part of the level, and all the lower regions of the mountains, are overgrown with wood, interfperfed with a charming variety of flowering fhrubs: many of the favourite denizons of our Englifh gardens, flourifh here in all their native luxuriancy. This dale terminates at Gedres, a rambling village on the fide of the mountain. The road is afterwards cut through the rock, and leads to a fituation that gave us an idea of confufion, and defolation, the effects of fome violent earthquake: the mountain is fplit and torn to pieces; its fides, and foot are ftrewed with innumerable huge blocks of ftone, detached from

C 2

the impending ridge that forms its bare fummit; the paffage through this rocky labyrinth opened to a magnificent amphitheatre; on the top waved thick forefts of firs, through which feveral ftreams forcing their way, dafhed down the lofty precipice, but almoft vanifhed away in mift before they could reach the bottom. The field below was beautifully overfpread with purple monkfhood.

Our morning's expedition ended at Gabarnie, where we found good accommodations prepared for us by a meffenger we had difpatched the preceding day. This is a village confifting of a church, and thirty houfes, in the midft of bare hills, fhaded by very high mountains, and traverfed in feveral directions, by foaming torrents. The curate partook of our dinner, after we had removed the table to the door of the inn, for he durft neither eat, nor drink, within the walls of a public houfe. We found him a modeft, converfable man, worthy of a richer fettlement. After dinner we travelled towards the head of the Gave, the object of our journey: we had long had in view the fnow-capped cliffs from which its waters iffue, but were furprifed to find them ftill fo diftant from us. We fpent an hour and a half in riding acrofs a bare tract of pafture, clofed in with immenfe forefts of evergreens on the French fide, and along the Spanifh frontier, which lies on the right hand, confined by bare rocky mountains: this plain is called the *Prade*; the river follows a ferpentine courfe through it: in winter it is generally covered with fnow forty feet deep. Not far from hence a filver mine was difcovered fome years ago, and worked by a company of adventurers; but the bufinefs was fo injudicioufly managed, and the conduct of the miners fo flagitious, that the miniftry thought proper to put a ftop to the undertaking. All the heights towards the fouth-weft, are debateable land between the French and Spaniards, and arbitrators have long been appointed to fettle the limits; but as they have hitherto made but little progrefs, the claimants have been under the neceffity of forming a temporary agreement to feed their flocks alternately upon the difputed grounds.

Our guide having now brought us to his *ne plus ultra*, preffed us earneftly to alight, as no horfe had ever advanced beyond this pafs: but as we were not contented with fo diftant a view, we rejected his timid advice, and clambering over feveral rocky eminences, plunged into the river, which by its limpidity deceived our eye, both as to the depth of the water, and the fize of

the

the rocks at the bottom. It required our utmoft exertions to extricate our
horfes, and bear them fafe through to the oppofite bank. This difficulty
being overcome, all others appeared contemptible, and we foon reached the
center of a moft ftupendous amphitheatre; three fides of it are formed
by a range of perpendicular rocks; the fourth is fhaded with wood : above
the upright wall, which is of a horrible height, rife feveral ftages of broken
maffes, each covered with a layer of everlafting fnow. The mountain caft-
ward ends in fharp pinnacles, and runs off to the weft in one immenfe bank
of fnow. From thefe congealed heaps the Gave derives its exiftence :
thirteen ftreams rufh down the mighty precipice, and unite their waters at
its foot. The whole weftern corner of the area below is filled with a bed
of fnow, which being ftruck by few rays of the fun at any feafon, receives
a fufficient volume of frefh fnow every winter, to balance the lofs occafioned
by the warmth of the atmofphere in fummer. Two of the torrents fell upon
this extenfive frozen furface; they have worn a huge chafm, and extending
from it, a vaulted paffage five hundred yards in length, through which their
waters roll. We boldly rode over this extraordinary bridge, and alighting at
the foot of the rocks, walked down the paffage. The fnow lies above it near
twenty feet thick; the roof is about fix feet above the ground, and finely turned
in an arch, which appears as if it had been cut and chiffelled by the hand of
man. In fome places there are columns and collateral galleries; the whole
glittered like a diamond, and was beautifully pervaded by the light. The
only inconvenience we felt, arofe from the dripping occafioned by the extreme
heat of the day, by which even this great body of fnow was ftrongly affected.
As we emerged with the river from this fingular grotto, we unharboured
three chamoy goats, that had taken refuge in the mouth of the cave, againft
the burning rays of noon: they darted acrofs the plain, and afcended the
fteepeft parts of the rocks, where we foon loft fight of them. Thefe animals
are called *Ifards* in this country; they are rather fmaller than the fallow
deer, of a muddy reddifh yellow colour, with fnubbed nofe, and fhort black
horns: in fhape they refemble a deer, walking with their heads upright, and
fkipping away with admirable fwiftnefs; but they do not bound; they run
when at full ftretch: no beaft of the foreft is of more difficult accefs; they
feldom quit the higheft and moft inacceffible parts of the mountains: during
the wintry ftorms, they have been feen fixed on the brow of a precipice, with
                                                                    their

their faces towards the wind, probably to prevent the rain and snow from lodging under their hair. Notwithstanding their suspicious, wild nature, and their extreme velocity, the hardy mountaineers find means to destroy them: they lie out whole days and nights watching their opportunity, and making good use of it, when it offers, for they are excellent markfmen: they have frequently as much difficulty in reaching the dead prey, as in approaching it while living. The flesh of the *Jfard* is much esteemed ; its skin makes soft and useful gloves.

The setting of the fun roused us from the ecstasy in which the contemplation of these awful scenes had enwrapped every sense, and warned us to retire, before the want of light should render those passes doubly dangerous, which we had found very difficult even in the glare of day. The fun sank behind the snowy cliffs in admirable beauty, tingeing the mountains with a rich variety of fiery hues, which died away into the most tender tints of purple.

The mountains abound with game, the rivers with fish: here are no lords or manorial rights, and therefore game is the property of every member of the community that can catch it. Except some tracts of wood reserved for the use of the navy, all the forests are held in common.

LETTER VII.

ON our return, we passed through the plain of Luz into a defile along a magnificent road opened by Monsieur d'Itigny, the late intendant of this province. This pass between two mountains clothed from top to bottom with dark woods, was extremely narrow, and the Gave rolled below with horrible noise, amidst rocks and cataracts. The way along the side of the mountain was either hewn out of the live rock, or formed by shelving down whole quarries of flate and shiver ; a parapet wall in the dangerous places diminished our apprehensions. At length the dell suddenly widened, the mountains retired on each hand, and our eyes were relieved, after so long confined a prospect, by the fight of the valley of Argillas, an oval plain of great extent, bounded in front by moderate elevations, beautifully planted and richly cultivated.

4

We

We then travelled up the courfe of another Gave, for three miles, to the mineral waters of Cauterets. This town ſtands in a wide vale, delightfully improved and planted: the furrounding mountains are thickly covered with wood ;* the wells lie in the midſt of a beautiful ſcene ; two vaſt torrents pour over a ledge of rock, ſhaded by an evergreen foreſt ; beautiful woody knolls rife behind, and mountains of great bulk feem to reſt upon them as upon a baſis: one of theſe hills is quite round, and an exact reprefentation of the eminence at the bottom of Ulfe water in Cumberland, called Dunmollin, which all perfons acquainted with our delightful lakes, eſteem a perfect model of rural beauty. Early on the 10th we returned from Cauterets to the plain, and took the road to Lourdes : this ancient caſtle is a confufed pile of towers and walls rifing in terraces, commanding the town and valley in a very grand manner, itfelf the nobleſt feature of the view : its ſtrong ramparts, though no longer eſſential to the defence of the country, are prefervod to confine delinquents of high rank.

From hence the journey down the Gave abounded with beautiful profpects : Lourdes long remained in fight, till hidden by towering rocks and hanging woods. We dined at Betharan, a place to which pilgrims refort, in great numbers, to pay their homage to an image of the Virgin Mary. The charms of its poſition, when known, would allure even an indevout traveller, delighting in rural elegance ; for nature has taken unufual pains to deck it out with her moſt feductive ornaments : a deep winding river, woody heights, and a fertile plain, unite in a rich foreground, while different ſhades of receding mountains compofe grand diſtances for the remainder of the picture. We continued our ride many miles, through one of the fineſt countries I ever beheld : the number of villages is too great to reckon, yet the fruitfulnefs of the plain feems to demand even more hufbandmen to gather in its productions. Coraffe lay near the road, an ancient venerable manfion, where Henry the Fourth was nurfed. Nothing can be more pleafing than the approach to Pau, the capital of the principality of Béarn, and the refidence of the kings of Navarre, after Ferdinand of Aragon had moſt unjuſtly wreſted Upper Navarre from them.

* The hotteſt fpring raifes the quickfilver to 118; in the cookeſt it falls to 69.

Pau stands on the brow of a hill, overlooking the immense plains through which the Gave meanders; its many streams join in one large body, before they pass under the arches of the bridge below: the southern horizon is bounded by a far lengthened chain of mountains, rising behind a range of well-wooded hills.

The royal castle built by king Henry of Albret, is situated on the happy point for enjoying the whole extent of this admirable prospect; its terraces communicate with a shady park, full of noble timber: neither the outward architecture, nor the interior decoration of this palace, merit any notice; nor do the apartments contain any curious tokens of their old inhabitants: the only relic preserved in it, is the shell of a tortoise, which the wardens assured us was the cradle of Henry the Fourth. The city consists chiefly of two long streets, but is destitute of ornamental edifices and public monuments; the only one I saw, was a bad statue of Lewis the Fourteenth, which presses a pedestal destined, as tradition informs us, for the figure of his grandfather, the glory of the house of Bourbon, and the darling hero of this province. The Bearnois seem to have been conscious how shocking it must appear to find no memorial of so good a prince in his own original patrimony, for the inscription says, " This is the grandson of our good king Henry."

The principality of Béarn is said by etymologists to have taken its name from the city of Bencharrica, once its capital, but now so completely destroyed, that nobody can ascertain where it stood. The Bearnois were in all ages men of an independent spirit, continually in arms to curb the growing power of their princes, and to maintain their native rights against encroachments. In the thirteenth century they insisted upon the sovereignty being elective, and though they did not succeed in that respect, they obtained a new body of magistrates, to be formed to control the authority of their prince. The ancient mode of government, though not the power, subsists in the states, which assemble annually to deliberate upon subsidies, and other concerns of the province: they are composed of the bishops of Lescar and Oleron, of whom the first is president of the meeting; three abbots, twelve ancient barons, four barons of less antiquity, and five hundred and forty gentlemen, possessors of fiefs, constitute the first branch of the states; the second consists of deputies named by forty-two towns.

Centul-

Centulphus was the firft fovereign of Béarn, and reigned in the tenth century : his pofterity for many generations paid homage to the kings of Navarre, or Aragon. The houfe of Foix acquired Béarn, by marriage, about the end of the thirteenth century; but in the fifteenth, an heirefs carried it into the family of Grailly, who affumed the name of Foix. In 1471, Gafton the Fourth procured the crown of Navarre for his defcendants, by marrying Eleanor daughter of John king of Aragon. Their grandfon dying without iffue, Catherine his fifter fucceeded ; her hufband, John de Albret, was ftripped of Upper Navarre by Ferdinand the Catholic. Jane daughter to their fon Henry, and wife of Anthony of Bourbon, was mother to Henry the Fourth, who afcended the throne of France upon the extinction of the houfe of Valois. This principality was not completely incorporated into the monarchy of France, till the reign of his fon Lewis.

The exportation from this province is inconfiderable, though fome of its wines are excellent, and proper for long voyages and foreign markets : thofe of Jurançon hold the firft rank ; they are extremely ftrong and heady. Coarfe linen is made in great quantities. The grain moft ufed for the nourifhment of the people is Turkey wheat: the plains abound with fruits, corn, and pulfe ; every neceffary of life is to be had at an eafy rate, and of a good quality. In the mountains, milk and cheefe fupply the place of many articles that are only to be found in the low country. Almoft every valley has its mineral fprings, and mines of various metals. The natives are an induftrious, ftrong, fhrewd, and lively race.

LETTER VIII.

A Ride of twenty-eight miles through rich vineyards and foreft lands, brought us to the city of Oleron, which is fituated upon the banks of two rivers, among beautiful hills. Its principal inhabitants are concerned in a lucrative commerce with the adjacent provinces of Spain, but it is not in fo flourifhing a condition as it was in the laft century.

On the 12th, we left our inn before day break, and in an hour's time

D entered

entered the ftreights that fhut in the valley of Afpe : this narrow glen is many miles in length, full of neat hamlets and cottages, and terminates in the large circular plain of Befouf, which is enlivened by the fcattered buildings of feveral villages, and thofe belonging to the king's maft-yards. From hence the road to Spain has been made by gunpowder, through a huge rock that hangs over the river. Seven miles further we came to the foot of the *Mature d'Efcat.* The mountains are here extremely lofty, rocky, and bare, except near their fummits, which are covered with filver firs. For the purpofe of felling and tranfporting fuch of thefe trees as are fit for mafts, the king has caufed a way to be cut in the flank of a frightful rocky mountain, that ftretches out over the bed of a very precipitate torrent : it is rather a chain of water-falls than a ftream. Every foot of the road has been gained by blafting ; in fome places where crevices in the rock have interrupted the folid communication, bridges are laid, fupported by huge beams driven into holes in the ftone, and thus fufpended over precipices, which the eye cannot meafure without horror. The ample breadth fcarce feems a fecurity againft the perils of this road, which is without comparifon the moft tremendous I ever ventured to climb. After a long fatiguing afcent, we were relieved by the levelnefs of a fmall plain at the head of the cataraçt, where the wood-hewers have built their huts. A large extent of wood has already been cleared, and the fupply of mafts in this foreft is nearly exhaufted. The trees, as foon as cut, are trimmed, and flung down with cables to a terrace near the foot of this upper range of the mountain. There each maft is faftened to ropes, and drawn by oxen down the road by which we afcended, to a tree of thirty-three inches diameter, the largeft fize this foreft produces : twenty four pair of oxen are yoked behind, to keep back the weight, and prevent the maft from rolling or fliding down with too much precipitancy ; yet the cattle are generally obliged to trot, fometimes very faft, fo prodigious is the weight and power acquired by the timber as it glides down. It requires great fkill in the drivers to guide their oxen at each turn of the mountain, to prevent the point of the tree from ftriking the rocks.

The felling and conveying of thefe mafts are performed by contraçt, at twenty-five fous per cubic foot ; but the king is bound to make the roads to Atas ; there the mafts are thrown into ponds, and afterwards let down into the river Gave of Oleron, faftened together in rafts: bundles of poles and planks defend them againſt the ſhock of the rocky ſhores, and ſcreens of wood are placed at every turn, to deaden the ſtrokes they muſt ſometimes give: eight men embark on board each float. It appears to me that the timber might be conveyed to the plain at an eaſier rate, were terraces contrived at different heights, to which the maſts might be lowered by means of cables and capſtans, as they are in the firſt inſtance, inſtead of employing ſo many oxen in the removal of a ſingle tree.

We returned by the valley of Aſpe to Pau, and from thence to Bagnéres, having made a tour of three hundred and twenty miles.

L E T T E R   IX.

Bagnéres, Sept. 2.

BEING deſirous of viſiting the Pic du Midy, I repaired early to Grip, at the head of this valley; from hence I aſcended to Tremeſaigues, a heap of hovels near the beautiful falls of the Adour, where I expected to meet with a guide, but not a man was to be ſeen ; all were out on the paſtures, tending their flocks, or wandering in the foreſt, in queſt of the Yſard. My reſolution was not damped by this diſappointment : I directed my ſteps towards a plain at the foot of the Pic. No buſhes grow upon this extenſive tract of paſture; ſhort graſs and low heath are here the ſcanty covering of the earth : a ſmall ſtream of excellent water iſſues from the bottom of the gigantic cone. Here I found a ſhepherd's boy, who engaged to guide me up the mountain. My ſervant and horſes remained at the ſpring head, while I followed my conductor up a rugged bank, between huge walls of ſhaggy rocks, where the melted ſnow pours down in torrents, on the return of ſpring. Rough and laborious was the aſcent, while the ſun, unobſcured by clouds, darted his rays perpendicularly on my head. By winding round to the ſouth ſide of the mountain, we at length arrived at the ſummit of a narrow ridge, which runs into the main body of the Pic, as wings are joined to a manſion by a gallery of communication. Not a drop of water was to be met with near the path, but I ſupplied the deficiency in ſome degree, by frequently applying a lump of alum to my tongue. I had now climbed up

D 2
nearly

nearly one third of the whole height of the mountain, from the place where
I had left my fervant, and enjoyed here an awful profpect down a vaft bafon
on the fouthern afpect, at the bottom of which lay a round lake: the water
was of a bright green colour. Before me an immenfe heap of black rugged
mountains rofe in fublime confufion, one behind another, till the horizon
was bounded by the fnowy table of Gabarnie. Not a trace of man or his
improvements was to be difcerned ; no tree, no paths, no animals ; all
dreary, filent, and favage. Here my guide refufed to proceed, affuring me
that neither he, nor any of his acquaintance, had ever ventured a ftep higher.
When I found that neither bribery nor expoftulation could remove his fears
and prejudices, I engaged in the adventure alone, and began to climb the main
body of the Pic : and now all my preceding toils appeared light, compared
with the difficulties I had to encounter in this afcent, which is fcarce to be
called a declivity, being fo near a perpendicular line : it juft affords flope
enough for a coarfe, flippery grafs to ftrike root, and ftop the fhelving fhiver
from being wafhed down to the bottom. Thefe tufts were my ftepping
places, without which it would have been impoffible to proceed, for the foil
flides away with a touch ; but the blades of this grafs are fo fharp and ftiff,
that they penetrated my efpartilles, or packthread fhoes, and often gave me
fuch pain, as to endanger my lofing my hold, and rolling down.

After numberlefs paufes I reached a fmall puddle of water, formed by the
melting of a neighbouring wreath of fnow, the only one left on the mountain : my thirft was exceffive, and I greedily fwallowed large draughts of
water, though it was hot, brackifh, and naufeous. I foon after gained the
fummit of the Pic, an entire flat, oblong rock, about thirty feet diameter,
inclining towards the fouth. From this pinnacle to the afore-mentioned lake
is one uninterrupted rapid flope : towards the northern and eaftern afpects
the rocks are perpendicular, and I believe, impervious to man, and beaft.
The Pic du Midy is a cone placed on the point of union of three inferior
mountains, by which it is fupported, as by a triangular pedeftal. I found
that I had employed near three hours in the afcent: the height of the mountain was meafured in the year 1740, by the Academicians, and determined
by the barometer to be 1441 toifes, equal to 9217 Englifh feet, above the
level of the fea. When I had refted my weary limbs, and recovered from the
difagreeable fenfations of exceffive heat, by expofing myfelf to a gentle breeze

that

that blew over the furface of this elevated rock, I ftrove to enjoy, as much as poffible, the charms of the moft extenfive and fuperb view the imagination can conceive, or the eye admit. To the fouth, fouth-caft, and fouth-weft, a line of innumerable mountains faded away into clouds at each extremity, where I thought, I could trace the outlines of both feas; but as the heat of the day had covered the very diftant objeƈls with a dim vapour, I may have been deceived, and only fancied I faw what I knew exifted in thofe quarters. On the northern afpeƈt lies a plain, confined only by the rotundity of the globe, and the inability of the eye to take in a greater proportion of its circumference: infinite was the variety of colours that enlivened its furface, among which none was fo gay as the golden hue of the ripe corn. I followed the direƈlion of the principal roads, traced the courfe of rivers from their head, and difcerned each town and city, that lies upon their banks: Tarbes, Aufch, and Pau were the moft confpicuous; but had I been provided with a good fpying glafs, I am confident, I might have diftinguifhed Touloufe, Montauban, and many other places equally diftant. I could not perceive the leaft diminution in my freedom of refpiration, nor any material difference in the degree of heat I felt there, and that I had experienced in the plain below, except what was occafioned by the fine zephyr, which cooled the air, and rendered the downright beams lefs irkfome. I lay an hour ftretched thus above the world, then feeling myfelf reftored to vigour, defcended to the plain in the fpace of an hour and thirty-five minutes. Thrift, blue-bottle, and meum, were the only flowers I faw on the higher cone: the plain abounds with pinks and dwarf-iris.

LETTER X.

Bagneres, Sept. 17.

I Laft week made an excurfion to Bagneres de Luchon. At Sainte Marie, above Campan, we turned to the fouth-eaft, along a delightful valley, furrounded by green hills and woody mountains. We baited at the Pas de Sude, in a fpacious plain in the center of noble forefts of filver firs: the lower branches

of

of thefe aged trees are thickly hung with long mofs, as delicate as flax. Beyond
this girdle of woods and mountains lies the valley of Aune, of which the
principal town is Arreou, fituated on the river Nefte, and completely hemmed
in by towering mountains. It was formerly reforted to by patients labouring
under nervous and fcrophulous complaints, which were frequently removed
by the ufe of a cold mineral bath: but Margaret queen of Navarre caufed it
to be filled up and deftroyed, out of refentment, as the popular tradition
goes, becaufe a favourite female attendant of hers, over whofe conduct fhe
had always watched with maternal folicitude, was debauched here, while the
queen was in the bath, the firft moment that fhe had loft fight of her. Had
we arrived at Arreou a day fooner, we might have partaken of the diverfion
of a bear-hunt; for that morning all the youths of the valley had affembled,
and killed a very large one, that did not yield till he had received eight fhots in
his body. The method of conducting this chafe, is to trace the animal to his
haunt by day-break; and as he never moves afterwards till night, the hunters
have time to collect their numbers, and furround the covert: the line of cir-
cumvallation being perfected, the game is roufed by the din of fifes, drums,
kettles, fhouts, and all manner of harfh and hideous noifes: aftonifhed and
terrified with this horrid ferenade, the bear rufhes out of the wood, to feek
fome more peaceable retreat; but as foon as he iffues from the thicket, the
difcharge of mufketry commences: if miffed, he runs upon the man that
fired, but repeated fhots call his attention to another and another object, till
one ball better aimed than the reft, difpatches him. Bears feldom attempt to
bite, but feek to annoy the enemy with their claws.

From Arreou we clambered over a dreary mountain, and then followed the
courfe of a rivulet down into the vale of Luchon. Bagneres de Luchon is a
fmall town, irregularly built, in the corner of a plain, which is about two miles
in diameter: the profpect is extremely circumfcribed, for the furrounding
chain of mountains is of great height: fnow lies all the year upon their
peaks. A ruinous tower on a pointed rock, ferved formerly as a guard to
the pafs into Spain, which is a gloomy, narrow dell, a mere crevice in
the mountainous line: were it not for this break, the boldeft traveller would
find it almoft impracticable to pafs this natural barrier of the two kingdoms.

The baths are at a fmall diftance from the town, and near the fprings which
iffue out of a rock: the hotteft bubbles up in a hole not a yard wide, and

its

its waters are as black as ink : the little pebbles at the bottom are incruftated with a filvery micatious fediment. Thefe fountains are three in number, varying materially in their degrees of heat, but all foapy and fetid, ftrongly recommended in cutaneous cafes. One of thefe wells is feparated, by a plank placed edgewife, from a copious ftream, which guſhes out of the fame cliff ; but inſtead of being hot and fulphureous, is the coldeſt and pureſt water in the whole valley ; their ftreams are fuffered to unite foon after, to fill the tepid baths.

We returned from Bagneres de Luchon by the plains, purfuing the courfe of the river Aune, down a rich dale to the village of Cierp, where the higher ridge of mountains terminates towards the north. At this point a landfcape prefented itfelf, which may claim a very high degree of pre-eminence among the fublime fcenes of nature : an amphitheatre of mountains, beautiful both in form and woody covering, clofe in the horizon on the fouthern afpeƈt ; a defolate caſtle, wildly fcated on a rock, varies the outline of the lower hills ; a fecond mighty chain of mountains on the eaſt fide is broken by a chafm lined with white cliffs, through which the Garonne iſſues majeſtically out of his native wildernefs, to flow henceforward without impediment, through rich and boundlefs plains, and to tranfport their produƈtions many hundred miles to the ocean. The river is even here of a noble breadth and depth, and carries barges of confiderable burden. Towards the north the valley expands on each hand, cultivation and population increafe, the mountains feem to draw back, and every thing announces a quick change from wild nature to the improvements of human induſtry.

Lower down, we paſſed in fight of Saint Bertrand, the capital city of the country of Comminges, fituated on a round knoll, backed by woody mountains. The ſteepnefs of the hill, the ferpentine courfe of the river, and the maſſy ſteeples of its cathedral, give it a ſtriking refemblance to the city of Durham.

This town takes its name from St. Bertrand its biſhop, who in 1100 built it near the ruins of Lion de Comminges, an ancient town deſtroyed in 585, by Gonran, king of Burgundy, for having received within its walls an impoſtor that pretended to be of the blood royal.

Our journey in the afternoon lay over immenfe heaths, clotted with oaks, to the ruins of Mauvefin, once a caſtle of ſtrength, erected by the Engliſh, to

overlook

overlook and defend the boundaries of their poffeffions. Near the foot
of the eminence on which this commanding tower rifes confpicuous on every
fide, ftands the Ciftercian Abbey of Efcaldiou, embofomed in woods; three
beautiful vallies meet at this point amidft rich meadows watered by the
river Larros. The monks enjoy an income of fifty thoufand livres a year;
the commendatory abbot has about ten thoufand. They are lords of feven
villages and a vaft tract of foreft, but derive fewer advantages from their
woodlands than might be expected, on account of the right each community
has of cutting the timber and coppice neceffary for its repairs and fuel: the
woodmen in this country plant out thick oak, beech, and chefnut trees,
about ten feet high and two inches in diameter, and firft cut off the heads.
Thefe trees grow aftonifhingly ftrait, lofty, and found, though expofed to
violent ftorms of wind and heavy falls of fnow. We foon after came to
a place where nets were fet to catch ftock-doves, which come from the eaft
about the time that the millet feed is ripe, and fly in large flocks after rainy,
hazy weather. Incredible numbers are caught during the feafon, which is
at the height in October. The time of our departure from hence is fixed for
the 22d inftant. We fhall quit this valley with regret, and long remember with
gratitude the pleafant hours we have fpent here.

The pleafures of Bagneres bear little affinity to thofe which are ufually to
be met with at the mineral waters in England; here are few affemblies, parties
of dancing or cards, and few great entertainments; the company divides itfelf
into fmall fets, and moft of the amufements are of a rural kind; the accommodations are comfortable, and the neceffaries of life good and plentiful.
The greateft inconvenience we have experienced, is the difficulty of getting
remittances of money.* Travellers muft either bring with them the fum in
cafh which they expect to fpend during their refidence here, or have it fent by
the carriers from their correfpondents at Bourdeaux, or Touloufe, an operation attended with expence and delay.

* Since I left the South of France, the inconvenience here complained of, has been effectually
removed by the judicious and extenfive plan fettled by Meffieurs Ranfom, Morland, and Hammerfley,
for accommodating travellers with money, in all parts of Europe: Bagneres and Bareges are
both comprized in their circle of correfpondence. Any perfon, who from bad health or curiofity
fhall be induced to vifit thefe remote provinces of France, may now procure from that houfe *circular
exchange notes*, payable to his order for whatever fum he fhall depofit in their hands; he will receive
the amount of thofe notes at any of the places mentioned in their lift of correfpondence, without
commiffion or charges, and at the *current ufance courfe of exchange on London*, at the time of payment.

LETTER XI.

Toulouse, September 24, 1776.

WE left Bagneres at the appointed time, and travelled to Toulouse along the banks of the Garonne.

Toulouse is an ancient city, which, like all places that boast of remote antiquity, has its origin and early history obscured with fables.* The Romans decorated it with many noble structures, but no other vestiges of them are left, than the brick arches of a small amphitheatre. It stands in the center of an extensive plain, which yields large crops of corn and millet; vineyards are scarce in the environs, and the wine they give is of a low quality.

The circumference of the city is about four miles: its streets are roomy, and houses well constructed; some of them are grand and spacious, but there is a gloominess in the colour of the brick with which they are built, and a want of motion in the streets, that casts a damp upon my spirits, and excites ideas of misery.

The manufactures of Toulouse are of small importance, nor is its trade considerable. The genius of the citizens inclines more to letters than to commerce; the law draws to it every person, that can amass wealth enough

---

* The Volsci Tectosages inhabited this part of Gaul at the time of the first Roman invasion in the 636th year of Rome. It continued to form a province of the Roman empire, till Honorius, finding himself hard pressed on every side by shoals of barbarians, endeavoured to save the main body of his dominions from destruction, by yielding a few distant members to some nations in preference to others, and thereby sowing dissention among them; with this view he, in 400, ceded the province of Narbonne to the Goths. In the eighth century they were subdued by the Saracens, who in their turn were driven back into Spain by Charles Martel, and his son Pepin. Charlemagne established earls at Toulouse, who soon after became sovereign princes; their posterity reigned four hundred years; but in 1208 Raymund the Sixth drew upon his head the vengeance of the Holy See, by assisting his subjects the heretics of Alby, against whom the Pope had published a Crusade. The chief of the holy confederacy was Simon de Montfort; he defeated the earl, and as the reward of his valour, received the earldom from the hands of his fellow soldiers: Amaury de Montfort, his son, being too weak to preserve his father's conquests, sold them to the king of France, who forced Raymund the Seventh to sign a treaty, by which he abandoned all his possessions, except the diocese of Toulouse, and that also eventually on failure of his issue. By the death of his only daughter, the earldom fell to the crown of France, in consequence of the aforesaid agreement.

E

to purchafe a feat on its benches: the church alfo fwallows up a large portion of the inhabitants ; poverty and idlenefs feem the lot of the inferior clafs. Nothing contributes more to check the fpirit of trade, than the temptation which the Capitoulat, or chief municipal magiftracy, holds out to every wealthy merchant: this office imparts the rank and privileges of nobility, not only to the perfons invefted with the dignity, but alfo to their defcendants, and is therefore the conftant object of ambition to every thriving father of a family ; when once attained, the channel through which the wealth flowed, is fhut for ever, and thus the plant is left to wither on its ftalk, juft at the moment when it began to acquire ftrength and juices fufficient to enfure a fucceffion of ufeful fruit. * Yet the Garonne prefents powerful incitements to commercial induftry, and Touloufe feems deftined by its fituation to ferve as a ftaple town between the upper and lower provinces, that line its fhores for many hundred miles.

The mills of the Bafade, with their wears, are a grievous impediment to the navigation of the river ; for goods muft be unfhipped and carried through the town, to be reimbarked above the falls, which occafions both expence and lofs of time. The ftates of Languedoc have endeavoured to remedy this defect, without deftroying the mills, which are effential to the purveyance of a city built in a plain, where windmills would remain ufelefs half the year, from want of wind. A canal has been dug to open a communication between that part of the Garonne which lies above the Bafade, and that which is below the dams, in order that loaded boats may pafs up and down the whole courfe of the river without interruption ; but the in-draught of the mill is fo ftrong, that few bargemen will venture to fteer for the upper mouth of the new cut, and therefore the fuccefs of the project remains problematical : a large marble baffo relievo of genii, feas, and rivers, is, however, erected to commemorate the era of this junction. It is alfo propofed to continue the work till it joins the laft bafon of the royal canal of Languedoc, which will facilitate the conveyance of merchandize not intended for fale in Touloufe.

The bridge over the Garonne, which is here 820 feet wide, is the work of Francis Manfard ; the ftyle of architecture is bold, but the holes which he has opened in each pier, to give an eafier paffage to the waters in great floods, are difagreeable blots in the mafs.

* Some families of high rank and great illuftration defcend from Capitouls.

The

The Touloufains are fo noted for devotion, that I was not furprifed to fee
their city crowded with churches, and half its extent occupied by convents
ftocked with many coloured inhabitants; but fanctity has been more predo-
minant than tafte for the fine arts; and although whole legions of faints are
here depofited in golden fhrines and marble tombs, fmall expence has been
beftowed in procuring good pictures or ftatues to reprefent thefe patrons and
protectors: it cannot here be faid that **the coftlinefs of the materials is eclipfed
by the excellence of the workmanfhip.**

Befides a regular army of priefts, friars, and nuns, Touloufe has a.fpiritual
militia, animated with equal if not fuperior zeal for the intereft of the church:
this corps confifts of a large number of laymen affociated under the denomi-
nation of penitents: kings, ftatefmen, and generals, have thought it an honour
to have their names enrolled on the lift; but times are altered, and I believe
men of fober judgment, and juft notions of religion, wifh thefe exercefencies
of the ecclefiaftical trunk were lopped off, rather than encouraged. Touloufe
has long been diftinguifhed for her unconditional fubmiffion to the dictates
of the court of Rome, and has too often cemented the connection with the
blood of human facrifices. This was the birth-place of the Inquifition;
and in our days, the proceedings that attended the condemnation of John
Calas prove that the feeds of the fanaticifm, which produced that cruel
tribunal, are not yet deftroyed in this province. The true ftate of this melancholy event is ftill hidden behind clouds of doubts and conjectures, nor
have I been able to procure any fatisfactory lights on the fubject. A fenfible,
uninterefted fpectator of the whole tranfaction affured me, that he had ftrong
reafons for fufpecting that John Calas had, by fome unlucky blow or pufh,
been the innocent caufe of his fon's death: the expreffions uniformly made
ufe of by that unfortunate parent, agree with this furmife.

The vaults of the Cordeliers are famous for the dried corpfes there depofited; but thofe preferved in the fubterraneous galleries of Naples, and Syracufe,
are lefs disfigured.

The church of the Carmelite nuns is neat; that of the Vifitation elegant.

The eight Capitouls affemble in a fpacious town-hall, faid to be the gift of
Clemence Ifaure, a learned lady and encourager of the liberal arts, who is
fuppofed to have flourifhed in the 14th century, and to have founded annual

prizes

prizes for poetry: thefe rewards are ftill diftributed by the academy of the Jeux Floraux, and confift in fprigs of gold and filver flowers. In the fame building is a gallery of portraits of illuftrious perfonages, natives of the province, but the fame of feveral that I faw there feems to be confined within the limits of its territory. The chronicles of Touloufe, which are fhewn here, have been regularly kept fince the year 1285; they contain many fingular traits of hiftory, and are embellifhed with miniature reprefentations of feveral public ceremonies; the entry of Lewis the Eleventh, while Dauphin, is one of the moft curious: in order to obtain for his mother the diftinction of a canopy, which the magiftrates refufed to grant her, he took her up behind him, and rode thus into the city, fharing with her all the honours paid to his own perfon.

Henry duke of Montmorency was beheaded in a court of this town-hall in the year 1632. He was a fpirited, popular nobleman, and, as fuch, an obftacle to the defigns of Cardinal Richelieu: by various artifices he was feduced into rebellion, defeated at Caftelnaudary, taken prifoner, and brought hither to meet his fate.

LETTER XII.

Montpellier, October 8, 1776.

BETWEEN Touloufe and Carcaffonne the country is difagreeably open, without wood or hedges; the towns and villages are placed on hills; the plains are arable, and through the middle of them runs the royal canal, which forms a communication between the Atlantic and the gulf of Lyons. It was executed under the direction of Paul Riquet, of Beziers, at the expence of eleven millions of livres, of which the king and the province bore equal fhares. The firft ftone was laid in 1667; and the canal opened in 1681, but it took many years to complete it. The length from Touloufe to Beziers, where it joins the river Orbe, is 125435 French toifes, equal to 152 Englifh miles. The fyftem of inland navigation has been fo much improved of late years, by the experiences and combinations made by fome fublime geniufes in that line of mathematics, that I make no doubt but this canal would be
fhortened

fhortened many leagues, were it to be undertaken afreſh. It is full of angles and turns that do not appear neceſſary; and on the contrary, in one or two places has been driven ſtrait at an enormous expence through numberleſs obſtacles, when a ſhort ſweep would have conveyed the waters, with greater eaſe and œconomy, to the place of their deſtination. There are fifteen locks upon it in the fall towards the ocean, and forty-five on the ſide of the Mediterranean. The higheſt point between the two ſeas is at Naurouge, which is elevated one hundred toiſes above the level of each ſhore. The canal is carried over thirty-ſeven aqueducts, and croſſed by eight bridges. To preſerve a conſtant ſupply of water near the centre in dry ſeaſons, a great baſon is formed at St. Ferreol, which receives the produce of all the ſprings that riſe in the black mountain.

The profits of this undertaking accrue from the conveyance of goods and paſſengers; the former pay by the league, the latter by the day. Three hundred and ſixty boats navigate the canal, and perform annually ſix voyages : the proprietors of the works receive a thouſand livres a voyage, which makes up a ſum total of two millions one hundred and ſixty thouſand livres ; the current expences and repairs amount to one million ſix hundred and ten thouſand livres, and conſequently there remain five hundred and fifty thouſand net profit, for the dividends. This account may perhaps fall ſhort of the truth, as there are always ſecrets in trading companies, which it is hard to dive into.

The dioceſe of Carcaſſonne, though far from a fertile country, is in a flouriſhing condition, and its inhabitants comparatively rich ; this good fortune is owing to the ſucceſs of its cloth manufacture. The woollen trade has long been attended to in this place, but in the laſt age the Dutch found means to ſupplant the French in the Levant, by lowering the price of drapery ; being themſelves able, by means of a large capital, to bear the loſs which this diminution occaſioned, as long as any rivality ſubſiſted. The reſtoration of this beneficial branch of commerce appeared to the ſagacious Colbert a taſk worthy of his comprehenſive and perſevering genius : he accordingly encouraged the attempts of ſeveral enterprizing citizens, and ſoon had the ſatisfaction of ſeeing a conſtant and lucrative mart for French cloths opened in the Ottoman empire : the manufacturers of Carcaſſonne have been acquiring freſh vigour every year ſince his adminiſtration : the trade that other nations uſed

ufed to carry on with the Turks has funk in the fame proportion. Towards
the clofe of the laft century, according to the information given by Mr. De
Bafville in his memoir, drawn up for the duke of Burgundy, the fum brought
into Carcaffonne in return for its exported woollens, amounted to nine millions and a half of livres. I am affured thefe looms now fend out annually
cloths worth fourteen millions, and furnifh the home trade with cloths to
the amount of two millions more.

This city contains fixteen thoufand fouls; it confifts of two parts, divided
by the river Aude; the high town ftands on a rock, furrounded with
antique walls, and defended by a venerable old caftle; the low town is regularly built in a fquare form. This place had once fovereigns of its own:
the laft earl, having fided with the Albigenfes, was ftripped of all his poffeffions, which were given to Montfort, and by that family transferred to the
crown of France.

From hence to Narbonne we travelled through a bleak country, extremely
unpleafant to the eye; the want of fhade, and the ftrong reflection of the fun,
render it intolerably hot in fummer; during the winter months, it is expofed
to fevere cold and high winds. The foil in general is rocky, or a red gravel.
The moft northerly olive-trees in France grow here. We firft defcried
the Mediterranean from the hills near Narbonne, which city ftands in a
low plain, expofed to inundations by its vicinity to feveral rivers that flow
towards the falt lakes.

We entered this city through a gate built with the fragments of Roman
altars, mutilated ftatues, infcriptions and trophies. The ftreets are narrow,
and an air of poverty reigns throughout. The church alone feems to engrofs
the wealth of the place; its archbifhoprick is numbered among the richeft
benefices in the kingdom; the palace of the prelate refembles the gloomy
fortrefs of an ancient feudatory prince, rather than the refidence of a French
archbifhop in thefe days of peace and elegance. Many fine remnants of
Roman fculpture, and literature, are preferved in the courts, and there the
Narbonefe may indulge their vanity in furmifes concerning the ancient magnificence of their city, whatever may be its appearance in its prefent reduced
ftate. Narbonne became a Roman colony 115 years before Chrift, and
gave its name to a large divifion of Gaul. The abode of proconfuls and pre-
fects, the mafters of the world, or at leaft their deputies, was fure to receive
every

every embellishment, and mark of diftinction, which thofe proud inhabitants could beftow : the pleafures of Rome were undoubtedly tranfplanted hither, and fumptuous buildings raifed for the fake of enjoying them. The numerous fragments, that occur in every part of the town, atteft the grandeur and tafte of its ancient decorations ; but time, and the fury of barbarians, have left none of thofe edifices ftanding.

The cathedral is remarkable for the loftinefs of its roof, but the ftyle of architecture is heavy. In the choir is the maufoleum of Philip the Hardy, fon of St. Lewis ; he died at Perpignan in 1285, while he was employed in defpoiling his excommunicated relation, Peter of Aragon, of his dominions.

Narbonne was formerly governed by fovereign vifcounts, but the kings of France acquired it in the 16th century. Its trade chiefly depends upon the exportation of its wheat, which is much efteemed for feed-corn, and, except olives, is the only important production of the diocefe; it is fent by a canal to the fea, where it is fhipped for thofe provinces along the coaft, that are deficient in that firft neceffary of life. The falt-pans on the lakes bring in a confide-rable revenue to the farmers of the revenue : the wafte grounds about Narbonne abound in aromatic plants, from which the bees extract a white and highly perfumed honey ; its gentle laxative quality recommends it to the apothecaries in preference to other honey.

The fields in the low grounds are divided by rows of mulberry trees, and mounds overgrown with thickets of tamarifks; the plough ufed here confifts merely of a flender handle, and a coulter, proportioned however to the light-nefs of the foil. Beyond this plain the country is mountainous, and dreary, as far as the banks of the Orbe.

We left the ftrait road to vifit the Mal pas, a paffage, where the canal of Languedoc is carried 147 yards through the heart of a mountain : the work is nobly executed ; a bold lofty arch is thrown over the water, to prevent the materials of the excavated hill from falling, and a parapet is raifed along the water edge for a towing path. While the workmen were opening this fubterraneous cut, they accidentally ftruck upon a channel made by the Romans, to drain a lake that once filled a vaft hollow on the fummit of the mountain. From the Mal pas to the furface of the river Orbe there is a fall of fixty-feven feet, which renders ten locks neceffary for the raifing or lowering the barges.

Beziers

Beziers commands a grand extent of prospect, but the ground is too bare of wood. The climate of this city is much celebrated, as well as the fertility of its territory : Vaniere often sings the praises of this his native spot, in his Prædium Rusticum, a didactic poem, which appears cold and dull to foreign readers, but has many charms for those persons that are acquainted with this country, and qualified to judge of the truth, with which he has penned his descriptions. The roaring winds that blow for a long continuance at different seasons of the year, are no doubt conducive to the purity and salubrity of the air, but their violence renders Beziers a very unpleasant place of abode while they last. The cathedral and the palace of the Bishop are admirably situated opposite to the finest part of the hills and a beautiful reach of the river.

The Romans, who perfectly understood the advantages of situation, sent a colony to Beziers; on the dismembering of their empire, it fell into the hands of the Goths; the Saracens dispossessed them, and fortified this post with great care. The obstinate resistance they made here against Charles Martel, incited that general to destroy the place after he had driven them out. Beziers rose from its ashes, and afterwards was governed by a race of independent sovereigns. In 1209 the viscount of Beziers joined his standard to that of the earl of Toulouse in support of the Albigenses ; this drew upon him the resentment of the Crusaders, who took his capital by storm, and massacred its inhabitants in great numbers, without distinction of sex or age. The kings of France soon after became possessed of the territory.

This is far from a commercial town ; nature is so bountiful to Beziers, and supplies it in such abundance with all the necessaries of life, that the inhabitants seldom feel any incitement to industry. 'Tis the sting of penury that rouses and inspires us with the daring spirit of mercantile enterprize. These people find enough at home to answer every purpose of their existence, and therefore neither trade nor manufactures are heard of among them. This is the account I received from various quarters, but were I to judge of the affluence of the citizens by their rueful countenances, and their ill-built, dirty streets, I should be tempted to write them down for the poorest set of men in the whole province. The diocese produces a great deal of oil, wine, silk, and corn.

After traversing a barren country some leagues in extent, we descended with great pleasure into the rich plains of Pezenas ; it is spacious, finely cultivated,

vated, and inclofed by hills dotted with fingle houfes and villages. Pezenas is not remarkable for good buildings; the number of its inhabitants is fmall. We foon exchanged the agreeable fcenes of this delicious plain for rocky mountains, bleakly piled one upon another, and productive only of fhrubs, which ferve for fuel. Near Loupian we came down to the edge of a large lake that communicates with the fea; the view here ftretches acrofs a noble bay; the branches of the olive tree and the vine hang over the waves, while diftant towns feem to float upon their bofom. The approach to Montpellier is uncommonly majeftic.

L E T T E R   XIII.

Montpellier, Nov. 1, 1776.

THE city of Montpellier covers a round knoll. Its walls are handfome and well preferved; they were built in 1208, by a fon of James, the victorious king of Aragon, to whom this prince had given the kingdom of Majorca and the earldom of Montpellier as an appanage. The fquare walk, called le Peyrou, upon the brow of the hill, is one of the grandeft in Europe; it is raifed upon feveral terraces, and adorned with a ftatue of Lewis the Fourteenth, a triumphal arch erected to the memory of the fame monarch, and a rotunda, in which fcrupulous architects will find little to admire: it ferves to receive the waters brought from afar, along a noble aqueduct of two ranges of arches, and is here mentioned with praife as the part of a beautiful picture. Nothing we find among the ruins of Roman grandeur can have a more fublime effect, than this vaft line of arcades ftriding over the hills and dales. The Peyrou commands a view of fea and land, that even draws the attention from its decorations; the lake of Magredonne is feen divided from the Mediterranean by a long ifthmus, through the middle of which the royal canal is continued eaftward from Agde; the boats upon it feem to be failing in the open fea; villages are fcattered along the edges of the lake, and the mountain of Cette towers beyond, like an ifland feparated from the continent by a broad channel.

F   The

The walks and other embellishments give the exterior parts of this city the appearance of a metropolis, but nothing within corresponds with this idea; for the streets are narrow, crooked, and steep; the houses, though solidly built, are plain, and without any striking ornaments of architecture. The number of inhabitants exceeds sixty thousand.

The states * of Languedoc assemble here every winter, and during the meeting Montpellier is a place of great gaiety; at other seasons the resort of foreigners gives it an air of life and activity, which is seldom to be met with, except in sea ports. Its climate has long been celebrated for whole-someness, and incredible numbers of invalids have visited it in hopes of relief from their complaints, or at least of finding an atmosphere more congenial to their delicate frames; but I suspect its merits have been over-rated, for in autumn and winter the winds are continual and very sharp; at the same time the sky is clear, and the rays of the sun powerful; therefore in every place sheltered from the north wind, the degree of heat is considerable, and perspiration excited by very moderate exercise: the cutting blast, which is felt at every corner, cannot fail of producing pernicious consequences to a body thus suddenly exposed with all its pores open. In summer, the influence of the marshes must be felt; indeed the faces of the people that inhabit the low grounds along the coast, bear sad testimony to the pernicious qualities of their air and soil; their hue is a dismal green, and agues harass them half the year. I have not yet seen a woman in Montpellier with a fine set of teeth; their decay is by some observers attributed to the effluvia of quicksilver, of which incredible quantities are employed by the surgeons; others lay the blame upon the vapours of verdigrease; but I incline to think that the proximity of the marshes is the principal, though not perhaps the sole cause.

The college of physic has long enjoyed great renown, and boasts of having taught or enrolled among its members many of the greatest physicians France has produced in the late and present centuries. Its privileges are extensive,

* The states are composed of three orders, the church, the nobility, and the commons; the first consists of three archbishops and twenty bishops; the second of one earl, one viscount, and twenty-one barons; the third of the deputies of dioceses, and magistrates of towns. Their business is to grant money to the king, to parcel out the contributions, to inspect the accounts of preceding years, and to watch over the privileges of the province.

and

and some of the most honourable are said to have been obtained by the favour of that wanton philosopher Rabelais, for which reason his gown is put on every new fellow by way of instalment. If the constant concourse of patients, and the best opportunities for acquiring the knowledge of simples, contribute to the increase of skill in a medical society, no school seems to have these helps in greater perfection than Montpellier; but of late years many sick persons have applied to other sources of health, and the consumptive English have been induced by fashion and the temptation of a milder climate, to breathe out their small remains of life on the warm shore of Nice.

Botany may be studied here with peculiar convenience, as the waste lands about the city afford samples of a greater number and variety of plants than can be found assembled in the same compass on any other soil in Europe. The king's botanical garden was first planned by Dulaurem, physician to Henry the IVth; it is well taken care of, and students are accommodated with every facility for acquiring the knowledge of vegetables. The gardener is wont to make an annual visit to the Pyrenean mountains, with a band of pupils, to examine the rare plants that grow in those elevated regions, and which are not produced in the plains and hills of Languedoc.

Perfumery, scented waters, and cordials of various sorts are prepared here with great skill; false cochineal, and a medicinal conserve, is made with the kermes, or gallnut of the holm oak; wax is blanched in considerable quantities; verdigrease * is the particular manufacture of this town; oil † and corn are sent out of its diocese in great quantities. It produces some excellent sorts of wine: fustians, and other cloths complete the list of its commodities.

---

* It is made by putting some quarts of wine in a large earthen jar; over the liquor are fixed cross sticks to bear a layer of raisins; over these is laid a thin plate of copper; this is repeated till the pot is filled; all air is then excluded for twelve days, by means of a thick straw cover. At the expiration of this term the copper plates are taken out, dried gradually in the shade, and then the verdigrease which has been produced upon them is scraped off.

† In December when the olives become black and shrivelled, they are beat down upon clean cloths, and carted to the mill, where they are thrown into a circular trough, in which a perpendicular stone turns. By the weight of this machine the fruit is crushed, and kneaded to a paste, then put into baskets of matting, with a hole at their top; these baskets are piled up under a press, and boiling water is poured upon them; the hot liquid brings out the oil, and carries it away with it into a tub, where the water sinks, and the oil is skimmed off with a ladle.

LETTER XIV.

Montpellier, Nov. 3, 1776.

MONTPELLIER did not exift, when Charlemagne deftroyed Maguelonne, a city built in the middle of the lakes, the retreat and bulwark of the Saracens. The bifhop and his clergy had already taken refuge at Suftantion, a village about a mile from the hill, where Montpellier was gradually formed into a town, by the concourfe of people that preferred this lofty fituation to the low country, both on account of fafety, and of health. From fome holy virgins, who either directed their choice, or did actually refide upon the hill, the new fettlement took the name of Mons Puellarum, the mountain of the maids. Maguelonne was, however, rebuilt in the twelfth century, but again finally abandoned in 1536, and the epifcopal fee fixed at Montpellier, which had belonged to the crown of France fince the year 1340.

The people of Montpellier took an active part in the rebellions that difturbed the reign of Lewis the Thirteenth, and diftinguifhed themfelves by their attachment to the reformed religion. The king befieged them in perfon, and having forced them to furrender, erected a ftrong citadel, to curb their refractory fpirit, and fecure their obedience to his authority. This fortrefs has been improved according to the modern fyftem of defence, and has often been of eminent fervice both to the monarch and the fubjects, in preferving internal peace, and keeping at a diftance the calamities attendant upon civil difcord, which defolated the other diftricts of the province.

The number of Hugonots is ftill great in this neighbourhood, notwithftanding the revocation of the edict of Nantes: perfecution has not had the full effect that was expected, and the milder arts of toleration begin to be put in practice; perhaps indulgence, and the allurements of ambition, may imperceptibly undermine that well-cemented edifice, which has refifted fo many open affaults and furious fhocks from the hands of priefts, and monarchs. Perfecution is no converter, and mild treatment can alone weaken the impreffions of education, and bring men to balance in their minds the weight of fpiritual opinions againft that of temporal advantages: when zeal abates,

as

as it foon will, if no longer animated by perfecution, indifference will quickly flide into its place, and extinguifh even the embers of that once outrageous fire. It is by thefe means that a long eftablifhed fect is extirpated. The fable of the fun, wind, and traveller, is perfectly applicable in the prefent cafe, and I make no doubt but the French miniftry have learned wifdom of their fabulifts.

From the rapid progrefs made of late years by the fpirit of toleration and humanity, it is to be prefumed that the torch of fanaticifm will never more be lighted up in our own country. It is time that the few remaining profeffors of the old religion of Britain fhould enjoy their obfcure lot in peace, and as they contribute doubly to the fupport of the ftate, be no longer excluded from that protection which it affords to all other diffenters, Chriftian, or anti-chriftian. The animofities of ancient parties fhould die with the families and interefts that gave them birth: the conduct of the king's Roman Catholic fubjects has been fo long uniformly loyal and peaceable, their numbers are fo fmall, and their impoffibility of giving any difturbance to government, were they even willing, is fo well acknowledged, that nothing feems better proved, than the propriety of knocking off the ignominious fetters with which they are ftill loaded: but in oppofition to this act of humanity, it is afferted, that their principles and doctrines are hoftile to civil and religious liberty. I fhall not enter into an argument on religious liberty, becaufe, it is certain, that the Roman Catholics will never have it in their power in Britain to force any man to go to mafs, and therefore no danger can accrue from their fentiments in abftract matters of faith. But, furely, it is the height of abfurdity to affirm that religion to be inimical to liberty, which is profeft by fome of the freeft people in Europe. There are cantons in Swizzerland, republics in Italy, and individuals in Corfica and Poland, as tenacious of their freedom as the moft ftubborn Briton can be; yet, they believe in tranfubftantiation, make the fign of the crofs, and acknowledge the pope to be the head of the church. Have we forgotten that we owe the ineftimable bleffings of juries to Alfred, who was fubmiffively attached to the papal authority? How often did not our barons and commons rife in arms, and fight for public liberty, before they had learned even to doubt of his infallibility, and furely the men that drew up Magna Charta were papifts. Let England remember, at leaft, that

that her Roman Catholics are neither intruders, nor innovators; but the
defendants of her old inhabitants, of those who for ages fought her battles,
and lavished their blood and fortunes in support of that glory and freedom,
of which their posterity is forbid to partake.*

Several of my mornings were devoted to rambles over the adjacent country; a fine extent of heath and forest, affords ample room for the most
eccentric wanderer, and the want of inclosures leaves almost every where
free passage through the vineyards and olive-grounds. The great variety of
plants, and the aromatic scents that rose under my footsteps, with the quick
succession of land and sea prospects, shifting as I moved up each hillock,
rendered me insensible to heat and fatigue. Near Perrol there are small
pools of water, impregnated with a strong vitriolic taste, and kept in constant
ebullition by the fixed air; they are used as baths. Near Saint George's I
strayed into a circular valley, exactly similar to the crater of a volcano, but
instead of being covered with purple ashes, and strewed with horrid lumps
of black lava, it was overgrown with arbutus, and other beautiful tall shrubs:
pleasant paths have been formed through the thicket by the shepherds, who
lead their flocks to browze under this evergreen shade.

The mountain of St. Loup, and the ruins of the castle of Monferrand,
seated on its most shaggy pinnacle, were the objects of another excursion.
St. Loup is esteemed one of the most elevated points in the front row of the
Cevennes, of which it commands a most extensive view. The lower region
is woody and romantic, the upper rocky; but the light in which it claimed
my attention was the probability, built upon its form, that a volcano had once
existed at its summit; a deep circular hollow near a mile in diameter, the
whole of it in tillage, is shut up to the north by a very high ridge of
rocks, which on the outside are so precipitate as to deny all access, but on
the inside slope easily to the bottom of the crater. The wall or crust towards
the south is much lower, and broken in one part; a breach that may be
perceived in every extinct volcano, being the passage effectuated by the over-
boiling torrent of lava, through the weaker part of the shell. The river Lers
bursts out of a cavern at the foot of this mountain, and immediately turns a

---

* These letters were written long before the 2d of June, 1780, but I cannot prevail upon
myself to strike out this passage, though it looks like a satire upon my country.

mill. The water is as clear as chryſtal, and its bottom entirely covered with graſs, which the cattle dive for and pluck up by the roots.

LETTER XV.

Nimes, Nov. 5, 1776.

LUND, the only place of note on the road to Nimes, is renowned for the excellency of its muſcadine wines.

Aiguefmortes appears in the marſhy plain to the right: the alterations occaſioned by the lapſe of ages in its harbour and neighbourhood, have furniſhed ſubject of meditation for many modern philoſophers, who have ſtriven to explain the natural hiſtory of our planet, and account ſyſtematically for all its wonderful changes and convulſions. Saint Lewis embarked at Aiguefmortes, for his expedition againſt the Muſſelmen: the communication was then open from hence to the ſea for large veſſels; but the kings of France, having ſoon after got poſſeſſion of Provence, where they were provided with more convenient ports than this, neglected Aiguefmortes ſo entirely, that its canals filled with ſand, and its haven became a ſedgy pool: the number of its citizens decreaſed annually from ſickneſs, or deſertion; the few inhabitants, that ſtill remain within its walls, are bribed to ſtay by the advantageous privileges which the town enjoys, and by the profits ariſing from the great ſalt-works of Peuais. The laſt event that figures in the annals of Aiguefmortes, is the landing of the emperor Charles the Fifth, in the year 1539, and his magnificent reception by his generous rival Francis the Firſt.

Nimes is a large city, built within a ſemicircular range of rocky hills: violent north-eaſt winds blow for many weeks after the equinox, without intermiſſion, and diſpel the unwholeſome vapours, which have been collected in this confined atmoſphere during the ſummer: all is open to the ſouth, as far as the Mediterranean, which is thought by ſome philoſophers to have waſhed the foot of the rocks of Nimes in ancient times; but this retreat of the waters muſt have taken place long before the Romans had extended thei conquefts to Gaul, as is evident from the obfervations of Pliny: that fagacious people would undoubtedly have availed themfelves of fuch an advantage as a harbour, had there exifted one at or near a place which they treated with diftinguifhed marks of predilection. A colony was fettled here by Marcus Agrippa, the fon-in-law of Auguftus [*]: fucceeding emperors took a delight in embellifhing Nimes with both facred and civil edifices; no place on our fide of the Alps retains fo many, or fuch perfect monuments of ancient tafte and magnificence, befides innumerable fragments, which have been made ufe of in building walls and gates in ages of barbarifm.

The amphitheatre is one of the beft preferved works of the kind now extant; its form is, as ufual, elliptical: [†] on the outfide are two orders, Tufcan and Doric, each of fixty arcades, divided in the firft gallery by pilafters, in the fecond by columns; above all is a battlement or parapet, that either formed the pedeftal of a third order, or crowned the fecond; perhaps the building was never raifed higher, for there appear at this height, which is fixty-eight feet from the ground, projecting ftones, bored through to receive the poles from which the awning was fufpended over the fpectators. Four gates gave admittance into the area, which is at prefent crowded with houfes. I was told that upwards of three thoufand perfons dwell within [‡] its walls, moft of them manufacturers, and profeffing the reformed religion. Above the houfes, the feats and vomitoria are ftill entire, as are alfo the mafks

> [*] As the coin ftruck in this colony exhibits a crocodile tied to a palm-tree, and the heads of Caius and Lucius Cæfar, fons of Agrippa, it is probable that the veterans who formed this fettlement, were drawn from legions that had ferved in Egypt and Syria, under the command of Agrippa, or his fons.

[†] The longeft diameter of the area meafures four hundred and fixteen French feet, the fhorteft three hundred and eighteen.

The fubftructions that fupport the feats and galleries are eighty-feven feet thick, fo that the whole diameter of the amphitheatre is one way five hundred and ninety, and the other four hundred and ninety feet.

I have followed the meafurement of Monfieur Cleriffeau, given with the plans and elevations of the monuments of Nimes, becaufe he is an architect, and either took the meafures himfelf, or copied them from the papers of the late Comte de Caylus. They do not thoroughly agree with thofe marked in other books.

[‡] The king has lately (1786) iffued an edict for deftroying thefe hovels, clearing out the area, and putting this noble edifice into proper repair.

and

and baſſo-relievos that adorned the keyſtones of the arches. The amphitheatre has ſuffered leſs from the wear of time than from fire, for Charles Martel is reported to have filled it with faggots, which he cauſed to be lighted, in hopes of deſtroying this ſolid building, which being turned into a fortreſs by the Saracens, had long refiſted his aſſaults, and coſt him numbers of his braveſt ſoldiers; but the blocks of ſtone were ſo maſſive, and the work ſo firmly put together, that the flames had ſcarce any effect upon it, except blackening the ſurface.

The temple, uſually aſcribed to the worſhip of Diana, ſubſiſts with half its ſtone roof yet remaining. It is of the compoſite order, but in a heavy ſtyle of architecture: the ſituation is picptureſque, on the brink of a large ſpring iſſuing out of the rock into a ſemi-circular baſon fifty feet deep; the waters are conveyed from hence through a public garden, in various channels, adorned with balluſtrades, vaſes, and ſtatues: this labyrinth of ſtreams is ſaid to be laid down as nearly as poſſible upon the ancient Roman plan. Numberleſs fragments of ornamental architecture have been found in cleaning the old canals, and copies of them employed in decorating the modern parapets. The ſtylobate, which probably ſerved as a common pedeſtal to a line of columns, has been imitated, and is much admired for the elegance of its running pattern.

On the ſummit of the craggy hill, that overhangs the city, ſtands the Tour Magne, a pyramidical tower of ſeveral ſtories, to each of which a winding ſtair-caſe afforded acceſs. The building contains below one large vaulted room of an irregular ſhape, with a conical roof; above it are ſix ſmall cells, round at the bottom like a kettle, with apertures only at top, and not communicating with each other. Antiquaries differ as to the uſe made of this tower, while ſome call it a public treaſury, others a granary, a third pronounces it to have been a light-houſe, and others a mauſoleum. The view from hence is delightful, comprehending the whole city, its almoſt boundleſs plains, the ſea, the mountains of Dauphiné, and the ſtill more diſtant heights of Provence.

G

L E T-

L E T T E R   XVI.

THE glory of Nimes is the Maison Quarrée, a barbarous appellation for one of the moſt perfect ſamples of an ancient temple, that the fury of barbarous conquerors, or ſtill more ſavage zealots, has ſpared. It is a temple of the Corinthian order, with ſix columns in each front, and nine on the flanks, the whole raiſed upon a baſement ſtory, five feet ſix inches from the ground. The columns on the ſides, and thoſe in the ſouth front, adhere to the wall; thoſe in the north front form a pronaos or portico, extending under the roof as far back as the fourth column ; here is the entrance of the temple, ornamented with pilaſters; the door was formerly the only opening through which light was admitted, but windows have ſince been broken in the ſide walls. * The exact meaſures are given below for the ſatisfaction of artiſts : for thoſe perſons who

	French feet.	in.
* Length of the whole baſement ſtory	108	
Breadth of ditto	34	3
Length of the temple and portico	81	6
Breadth of ditto	42	6
Outſide length of the temple, with the portico	53	6
Outſide breadth of ditto	37	9
Inſide length of ditto	48	10
Inſide breadth of ditto	32	6
Thickneſs of the walls	2	10
Diameter of the columns	2	8
Diameter of their baſe	4	0
Intercolumniation of the ſides	5	0
Height of columns baſe	2	6
ſhaft	23	0
capital	3	2
Height of pediment	14	9
Breadth of the door	10	2
Intercolumniations of the front	5	4
	4	9
	4	10
Height of the baſement and ſteps	5	6
Height of architrave	2	3
Ditto of frize	1	9
Ditto of cornice	2	3

are

are not converfant in the rules of architecture, it will fuffice to fay that the
elegance of proportion, the exquifite tafte difplayed in every ornament, the
lightnefs of the whole building, and the harmony with which all the parts
are connected, ftand unrivalled by any work of the moft refined art north of
the Alps; but I do not think it is entitled to rank before every edifice that
ftill perpetuates the glory of ancient architects in Italy, Greece, and Afia.
It is apparent from the holes by which the brazen letters were faftened to
the ftone, that there was once an infcription on the frize, torn down for
the fake of the metal. The words of this infcription had remained a myftery,
never fatisfactorily explained by any antiquary, when Monfieur Seguier, of
this city, thought of tracing the form of the letters by means of the relation
which the holes bear to each other : the following lines were the refult of this
ingenious procefs.

C.C.AES.AR.I.A.V.G.V.S.T.I.F.C.O.S.L.C.A.E.S.A.

R.I.A.V.G.V.S.T.I. F.C.O.S.D.E.S.I.G.N.A.T.O.

P.R.I.N.C.I.P.V.S.I.V.V.E.N.T.V.T.I.S.

From this difcovery he drew an inference that the temple was erected in
the reign of Auguftus, and was not a monument raifed by Adrian to the
memory of Plotina, as moft preceding antiquaries had believed it to be.

Being convinced of the truth of his hypothefis, he fupported it by the following arguments: the Pantheon built by Agrippa fhews us that every thing
beautiful in architecture was to be expected from the genius of the artifts of
that age, and the magnificence of the great men that employed them : the
Maifon Quarrée is a moft admirable piece of ftructure, and therefore may
with ftrict propriety be affigned to that æra ; the names both of Agrippa and
of his fons were probably held in high veneration by a colony to whofe fettlement and profperity that general had contributed fo effentially ; nor could the
Nemaufenfes pay their court more effectually to the emperor, than by honour-
ing as divinities thofe youths whom he looked upon as the pillars of his
imperial houfe ; but from the total change of interefts and affections in the
fucceeding reigns, it would have been the height of imprudence afterwards
to have paid this homage to Caius and Lucius Cæfar ; and for that reafon,
the infcription being explained as above, the temple could not be dedicated
later than the time of Auguftus.

Thefe

These are plausible arguments, but in my opinion, there are others to be deduced from internal evidence, that completely overthrow them. By the comparison which I draw between this building and the undoubted monuments of the Augustan age, I am fully persuaded that they are not coeval, but that the space of, at least, a century intervened between the different epochas of their erection. In the Maison Quarrée I perceive a profusion and minuteness of ornaments not to be found in the more simple architecture of the Augustan times; there is also a great variation in the proportions. The explanation of the dedicatory inscription given by Monsieur Seguier, would have had more weight with me, had I not seen clearly that the disposition of the holes was not always uniform upon a repetition of the same letter; and that there were also several supernumerary ones, of which he made no use in placing his letters: he accounted for this redundancy by supposing them to be what painters call *pentimenti*, or mistakes which the workmen afterwards rectify by cutting others. The inside of this elegant structure has been repaired in a bad taste, in order to accommodate it to the purposes of the Christian worship: the Augustinian friars are the present possessors; and this adoption has preserved so valuable a relick of antiquity from the ruin which has overwhelmed so many magnificent edifices.

Monsieur Seguier embraces almost every branch of the polite arts as well as of natural history, and by his extensive acquirements in science, comes near the idea of universal knowledge; with these merits he unites the most unaffected politeness and pleasing communicativeness. We experienced this amiable disposition during a long stay in his Musæum, which contains many fine assortments in natural history: the most complete and singular, is a collection of plants and fishes impressed upon a black, slaty, fossile substance.

LETTER XVII.

WHILE the Roman government retained its vigour, Nimes continued to flourish as one of its most favoured transalpine settlements: the Antonines, whose family is supposed to have belonged to this colony, patronized

ized it in a diftinguifhed manner; but when Rome fank beneath the weight of thofe torrents of barbarians that poured upon her from the forefts of the North, Nimes was one of the firft cities that felt the fatal effects of her debility; its riches allured each rapacious invader, and repeated devaftations foon laid its glories in the duft. Nimes had fuffered fo much when the Vifigoths obtained poffeffion of this part of Gaul, that they gave the preference to Touloufe for the refidence of their monarchs: they converted Nimes into a frontier garrifon, built towers upon the amphitheatre, and, overturning moft other monuments of elegant tafte, employed their fragments as materials of defence, without paying the leaft attention to their beauty. The amphitheatre thus metamorphofed flood feveral fieges, each of which contributed fomething towards disfiguring it. Under the Carlovingian kings, vifcounts were appointed to keep the country in due fubjection, but they foon took advantage of the decline of that royal houfe, to affume independence: from them the fovereignty of Nimes paffed to the earls of Touloufe, and followed the fate of their other dominions.

The reform of Calvin was early introduced into this city, where it ftruck deep and vigorous root; the Hugonots lived here in a manner independent of the regal authority, till Cardinal de Richelieu fubdued them. A very large proportion of the Nimois, and of their immediate neighbours, ftill profefs the proteftant religion; to which they and their forefathers have adhered upwards of two hundred years with unremitting zeal, in fpite of all the efforts of priefts and monarchs. In the general wars of religion, they bore an active part, and alfo frequently rofe up againft government, when the reft of France was in profound peace.

The troubles of the Cevennes in the beginning of this century filled this part of Languedoc with bloodfhed and defolation. The proteftants, whofe imaginations were exalted to a degree of frenzy by the preaching of their prophets, and the fenfe of their own diftrefsful fituation, made no fcruple of exercifing the moft fhocking barbarities upon their enemies and perfecutors: on the other hand, the king's officers and foldiers retaliated thefe outrages, not only upon the Hugonots taken in arms, but alfo upon the whole body of peaceable inhabitants profeffing that doctrine. A difpaffionate reader of fuch narratives is apt to accufe the hiftorians of each party of monftrous exaggeration, humanely thinking that favage beafts alone are capable of perpetrating fuch deeds of blood.

But

But the crimes of that war lofe their blacknefs, if compared with the cruelties of the *Michelade* in 1567, when the Calvinifts fuddenly took up arms at Nimes, and made a general maffacre of the catholics. This atrocious fact has been alleged in alleviation of the *Saint Barthelemi*, which happened five years afterwards ; but there can be no juft parallel drawn between the fudden though outrageous fanaticifm that feized the Nimois, and led them to cut the throats and deftroy the property of their fellow citizens, and the cool, premeditated plan of Charles the Ninth, founded upon the bafeft treachery and hypocrify, under the fanction of oaths and facraments.

After the revolt of the Cevennes was quelled in 1705, this province was fuffered to enjoy fome repofe, but proteftant conventicles and preachers obtained no further degree of toleration : marriages contracted between proteftants continued to be deemed illegal and invalid ; their meetings, though held in the moft retired parts of the country, were difturbed by attacks from the civil and military power, and many of their minifters yearly hurried to the gallies. Of late years a greater latitude of indulgence has been given ; the troops affect to miftake the place of rendezvous, or previous notice is fent to the affembly. The benevolent fpirit of Lewis the Sixteenth will probably incline him to pafs fome law, by which their marriages may be rendered legal, and the birthrights of citizens be extended to their offspring.

The diocefe of Nimes is extremely fertile in corn, wine, oil, and other valuable productions. The inhabitants of the epifcopal city, in number above forty thoufand, apply with great induftry to commerce, efpecially that of filk : their manufactures would flourifh ftill more, could they be freed from numberlefs duties and oppreffive monopolies, which at prefent harafs the trader, and check the fpirit of enterprize. Catherine of Medicis is faid to have introduced filk-worms into France ; but the firft eftablifhment of a filk manufacture appears to date no higher than the reign of Henry the Fourth, or his fon Lewis the Thirteenth.

L E T T E R   XVIII.

WE are juft returned from an excurfion to Arles, where the beauties of fituation, and numerous remains of antiquity, made us ample amends for our fatigues. We travelled part of the way in a rich plain, where a great number of fowlers were ftationed, turning fmall mirrors in order to dazzle the larks, and draw them down within reach of their guns. A range of gravelly hills then intervened between this flat country and the boundlefs levels that line the courfe of the Rhone. We ferried over a branch of this river into the ifland of the Camargue,* and then paffed by a bridge of boats into Arles, which rifes nobly from the water edge up a gentle acclivity. Its circumference is not great, nor the prefent population numerous; the appearance it now makes is widely different from what it was, when Conftantine the Great, and after him his fons honoured it with their prefence. Then theatres, palaces, and amphitheatres were raifed on every fide, to receive and entertain thefe mighty guefts, and Arles became the center of government, the rival of Marfeilles in the trade of Italy: thither the inhabitants of the northern diftricts came to purchafe the gaudy fuperfluities of luxury, and from thence carried back into their forefts, new wants and the vices of more refined nations. The urbanity which a fplendid court is wont to diffufe around the place of its refidence, polifhed the manners of the Arelatians to a fuperior degree above the citizens of other towns; and if I may credit the report of travellers, who have remained there long enough to form acquaintances, this foftnefs of manners, and eafe of behaviour, are ftill perceptible in the focieties of its nobility; holding a pleafing medium betwixt the formality of the long robe, that leads the fafhion at Aix, and the familiarity, which at Marfeilles is acquired by habits of traffick.

The glory of Arles faded with that of Rome; and from the day that Honorius fubmitted to the dictates of the barbarian powers, this city became involved in continual difquietudes and diftreffes; befieged, plundered, depo-

---

* The Camargue is an ifland eighteen miles in length, formed by two branches of the Rhone. It is extremely fertile, and feeds an incredible number of horfes and cattle which are almoft wild. The horfes are active and hardy, but unruly and ugly.

4

pulated, by every paffing fwarm of conquerors, it fell to ruin, commerce fled from its deferted wharfs to feek profperity in other ports; the canals that were wont to beftow fertility upon its fun-burnt plains, and to convey their rich productions to a ready fale, were left without repairs or fupport, and foon choaked up with fand, forming heads to numberlefs torpid pools, the nefts of infection and difeafe.*

Arles thus abandoned to mifery, languifhed many centuries, but even at its moft difaftrous period, while its ruined edifices were yet reeking with the fire which the Saracens had kindled, Bofon, the brother-in-law of Charles the Bald, chofe it for the capital of a kingdom which he had erected out of many ufurped provinces. After paffing through two families, this title devolved upon the imperial houfe of Swabia, a great but unfortunate race of princes, that failed in the year 1268. Long before this epocha their power in Provence had been reduced to an empty name; for on one hand the earls of Provence had ufurped whatever territory lay convenient for them; and on the other, feveral of the moft powerful cities had, in imitation of thofe of Lombardy, caft off the yoke, and formed themfelves into republics. The people of Arles afferted their independence about the year 1220, and chofe annual podeftats to govern them.—At the end of thirty years this infant and ill-eftablifhed commonwealth was obliged to fubmit to the authority of Charles, the firft earl of Provence, of the houfe of Anjou, too formidable an antagonift to be refifted with any reafonable hopes of fuccefs. The kings of France fucceeded in later times to the rights of the earls of Provence; and the emperor Charles the Fourth made over to his nephew Charles the Fifth, king of France, all the claims he might have upon Arles and its territory.

The ftreets of this city are narrow, but the houfes in general are well built; it abounds in rich clergy and poor nobility: trade feems at a low ebb.

In the fame fquare with the cathedral and the archiepifcopal palace, ftands the town-hall, a fhewy infulated building; its ftaircafe is ornamented with pieces of antique fculpture and the caft of a female figure, which was dug up here in the laft century, and furnifhed matter for many differtations, tending to afcertain the divinity it was meant to reprefent; the ftatue was fent to

* Since the French monarchs have poffeffed Provence, thefe evils have been in fome meafure remedied; but there are yet many parts of the environs of Arles that are exceedingly feverifh and unwholefome in fummer.

Ver-

Verfailles, where Girardon the fculptor made a Venus of it. A votive altar infcribed to the Bona Dea by her prieflefs, is remarkable for an oaken crown, that furrounds the infcription, and two human ears with ear-rings. The apartments are noble; in one is a fine portrait of Cardinal de Richelieu.

Many infcriptions are alfo preferved at the archbifhop's, and before his gate ftand a mutilated column, and an Egyptian obelifk of grey granite, without hieroglyphics; it is forty-feven French feet high, on a bafe raifed feven feet from the ground, and is fuppofed to have been brought from Egypt about the year 354, when Conftantius celebrated the Circenfian games at Arles with great magnificence. It lay buried in rubbifh many ages, till a reviving tafte for the arts brought it out of its obfcurity in the fixteenth century, but it was not raifed till the year 1676, when it was placed upon a pedeftal with great ceremony, and loaded with a moft flattering infcription in honour of the king.

In the herb-market two pillars, the remains of a portico, yet fupport the angle ftones of a Corinthian frize much broken; by the help of holes cut upon it, Monfieur Seguier has difcovered that the building was erected in the time of the firft Chriftian emperor. The only remnants of the theatre are two compofite columns belonging to the fide of the ftage.

The amphitheatre is of a fmaller dimenfion than that of Nimes, but, like it, is disfigured by the miferable dwellings of the poor: it never was finifhed, the work having probably been interrupted by the prohibition iffued againft gladiatorial fhews foon after Chriftianity afcended the throne of the Cæfars. Through a ftrong attachment to thofe fanguinary entertainments tranfmitted from father to fon fince Provence belonged to the Romans, or at leaft, fince it was fubject to the kings of Aragon, the people of Arles retained the tafte for bull-feafts down to the prefent age; wild bulls were frequently driven from the Camargue, and combats exhibited in the ancient amphitheatre before a vaft concourfe of fpectators, who were agitated by the fame fierce emotions, and expreffed them with the fame frantic acclamations, that refounded in the fhews of ancient Rome, and are ftill to be heard in the bull-feafts of Spain. The frequent lofs of human lives induced government to abolifh thefe favage fports at Arles.

This amphitheatre confifts of two orders or ftories of arcades, divided below by Tufcan pilafters, above by columns, of which the order cannot be difcovered, as their upper part is wanting: all the fhafts are lefs imperfect at the fame height, and the fixty arches of this ftory remain without any ftone work above them, which proves beyond a doubt that the building was never finifhed. There is no trace of feats, podium, or other interior works neceffary for an edifice of this kind; it is placed on an eminence, and the architect has excavated the hill in fuch a manner as to form a fubterraneous or bafement floor, by means of vaft galleries, halls, and receffes, which are either cut in the rock, or built with fquare ftone. The entrance into this dark labyrinth is in the fide of the hill: it is not eafy to give a rational guefs at the ufe of thefe vaults, which have no communication with the upper ftories; they probably were intended for magazines and cellars.

Without the walls of the city is a rocky hill called the Elifcamps, almoft wholly covered with ftone coffins, in fome of which were depofited the afhes of pagans, in others the bodies of Chriftians: the adjoining church belonging to the Minimes, is full of ancient farcophagi, funeral infcriptions, and figures: one fmall maufoleum remains on the hill, with fome of its colombaria or niches, wherein the urns were placed, yet entire. In the midft of the cemetery, an obelifk marks the grave of four confuls of Arles, victims to the plague of 1720, which from Marfeilles fpread its deftructive contagion, though not with equal fatality, along the coaft of the Mediterranean, and into the inland diftricts of Provence.

We were delighted with the drefs of the women we met returning from market; it reminded us of the airy garments upon the dancing nymphs of Herculaneum. Thefe peafant girls wear light, open mantles, loofely flowing to their knees, over a fhort petticoat, that difcovers their taper legs and filk ftockings; bracelets of gold beads adorn their wrifts; a filk handkerchief confines part of their jet black locks, without hiding their keen eyes and animated countenances: this eafy habit fuits admirably with the elegance of their form and the fupplenefs of their limbs.

L E T-

L E T T E R   XIX.

Avignon, Nov. 10.

REMOULINS is the firſt port from Nimes, and near it the river Gardon has worn itſelf a deep bed in the heart of a wild, mountainous country; the ſides of the dell through which it flows are joined together by a bridge of three rows of arches, one above another, built by the Romans to ſupport an aqueduct that conveyed the waters of two ſprings from Uſez to Nimes. Many fragments of this aqueduct, which was above ſeventeen miles long, are ſtill ſtanding in various parts of the hills. The above-mentioned bridge, known by the name of the *Pont du Gard*, is entire. The loweſt ſtage or order reſts upon the rock, and contains ſix arches, to which a collateral bridge was added in the year 1747, wide enough for carriages. The ſecond row is compoſed of eleven arches, ſix of which are perpendicular to thoſe of the firſt; a conſiderable part of the piers of this middle order had been ſcooped out to afford a paſſage for horſemen, but when the bridge below was doubled, this way was built up. The uppermoſt range conſiſts of thirty-five arches, and above it is the channel for the water covered with large flags.*

The only inſcription yet diſcovered conſiſts of the four letters A. Æ. A. which have occaſioned a great variety of opinions and explanations among

* Meaſures.

Loweſt Row.		
Diameter of the arches	58	French feet; the middle one, under
pillars	18	which the river paſſes, is 70 wide.
Height	83	
Height of parapet	8	
Middle Row		
Diameter of the arches	56	
of the pillars	15	
Height	67	
Height of the parapet	6½	
Uppermoſt Row		
Diameter of the arches	17	
pillars	5½	
Height	32	
Height of the channel for water	3½	

the

the learned. * Some attribute the work to Agrippa; others to Adrian, and others to the Antonines: it certainly does not belong to a later period, for its folidity, juftnefs of proportion, and fimplicity of ftyle, are too ftriking to leave a fufpicion in our minds that it could be defigned or built by the artifts of fubfequent ages. While I contemplated this ftupendous pile, ftretching fublimely from rock to rock acrofs the valley, and the broad ftream of the Gardon rolling with eafe through its wide arches, I felt my mind ftrongly impreffed with veneration for thofe extraordinary men, who had the fpirit to plan, and the force to rear fuch coloffal monuments of their art. No diffi-culties could difmay them, none could occur that were not removed by their perfevering efforts; the life of a Roman foldier was fpent in continual toils; his victorious hands, that had bowed the ftubborn barbarian to the yoke, were afterwards employed in fecuring the tranquillity and obedience of the conquered province, by raifing ftupendous mounds and fortifications, or in procuring with incredible pains the conveniencies and luxuries of life for the fettlements eftablifhed within them : fcarce is there a corner of the world, which was known to the ancients, where the traveller does not to this day, meet with ftately memorials of their indefatigable and elevated genius.

Soon after quitting the vale of the Gardon we reached the top of the hills, from which we overlooked the whole Comtat Venaiffin, and the city of Avignon. The Rhone itfelf is fo broad and majeftic a ftream, that it fuffices alone to give dignity to a landfcape; the awfulnefs of an immenfe plain terminated by the blue mountains of Dauphiné, excites fublime ideas, and rivets the attention upon the general effect of fo vaft a fcene, without fuffering it to wander, and wafte itfelf on minuter lights flowing from the various objects that compofe it.

A grand monaftery of Benedictine monks at Villeneuve commands a nearer view of the river and city. At every ftep we advanced as we defcended the hill, new beauties of profpect difplayed themfelves, till at laft we reached the banks of the Rhone, where a venerable old tower nods over the moft rapid of currents.

---

* Not one of the applications that I have feen agrees with thefe initials; thofe who read the name of Ælius Adrianus in them did not know that Adrian is always written on his medals with an H. Perhaps it may be decyphered thus, *Aqueductum Ædificabat Agrippa.*

Here once was fixed the extremity of the bridge of Avignon, begun in the year 1177 at the folicitation of Benezet, a young thepherd, who pretended a miffion from heaven for collecting alms towards building a bridge acrofs the Rhone. The legend fays that he enforced his preaching by miracles, and raifed fuch a fum as proved fufficient not only to complete that undertaking, but alfo to endow a hofpital, and create a fund for the future repairs of the bridge. Whatever we may think of the miracles of this young architect, the chronicles of Avignon atteft the reality of his exiftence : perhaps the artful magiftrates, feeing the neceffity of a bridge, and confcious of their own inabi-lity to erect one, brought forward this pious artifice to captivate the benevo-lence, and excite the generofity of a devout and unenlightened age. This bridge was the boaft of the country, but the Rhone has long torn down and buried in its whirlpools the greater part of it ; at prefent a perilous ferry affords the only accefs from the weftern fhore.

LETTER XX.

AVIGNON is about three miles and two furlongs in circumference, furrounded by handfome battlemented walls and turrets, not unlike thofe of Rome; its ditches are fhaded by pleafant avenues of elms. The number of inhabitants is not proportioned to the extent, for it amounts only to thirty thoufand fouls, of which above a thoufand are ecclefiaftics, and fome hundreds Jews. From the oppofite hills this city feems a foreft of fteeples, the bells of which are never at reft ; by day and night fcarce a minute can be counted undifturbed by fome bell or other, either roufing the monks and nuns to their duty in the choir, or giving the more welcome fummons to their repafts ; this inceffant tinkling made Rabelais call it the *Ifle fonnante*, an appellation I felt all the force of during every night of our ftay. One of thefe bells is of filver, and rung upon no occafion but the death of the Pope. Clergymen and friars fwarm in the ftreets, as may well be expected in this little Rome, but they have not brought with them the Roman tafte in building and decorating either their own abodes, or the temples of the divinity. The ftreets are nar-

4 row

row and dirty, as muſt needs be the caſe, where all manner of filth is emptied out of the windows: the diſmal lanes, in which the Jews are ſtyed, are abſolute ſinks of naſtineſs and infection: nothing leſs than the fierce and ſteady winds that predominate here for many weeks at a time, could purify ſo fetid an atmoſphere, and preſerve the town from plagues, and epidemical diſeaſes.

The public edifices are large, ſolid, and as grand as the taſte of the age could make them, for moſt of them were built in the fourteenth century, while the Popes reſided here; they occupy the moſt elevated point within the walls; the cathedral is ſmall and dull, offering nothing to the curioſity of the traveller, ſave a ſilver altar, many coſtly veſtments, and the tombs of Pope John the Twenty-ſecond, and Benedict the Twelfth *. The church of the Cordeliers is noted for the boldneſs and loftineſs of its roof, but much more for the tomb of Petrarch's Laura, who during her life, and after her deceaſe, received the tribute of his muſe in more copious numbers than were ever inſpired by any ancient or modern fair one: he ſang her charms, and his love, in four hundred ſongs or ſonnets. Petrarch is claſſed by the Italians in the firſt rank of poets, rather on account of the purity of his language, and the terſe propriety of his expreſſion, than either the originality and fire of his imagination, or the variety of his ideas: ſo greatly do his merits depend upon the manner in which he has clothed his thoughts, that it requires great habit of the Italian tongue to feel their value, and therefore few foreigners can taſte his beauties in the original, or admire him when tranſlated. Laura and her huſband, Hugh de Sade, reſt in an obſcure corner of the church, under a monument diſtinguiſhed only by an obliterated ſcroll, and a mullet, which was the arms of the family. Francis the Firſt, himſelf a poet and a paſſionate admirer of the fair ſex, cauſed the tomb to be opened in his preſence, and having read the verſes Petrarch had depoſited with the remains of his adored miſtreſs, cloſed down the lid, and inſcribed it with ſome lines of his own compoſition. Another gallant and rhyming monarch, René of Anjou, has left many productions of his at Avignon, both in poetry and painting, but they are more curious on account of their ſingularity, than of their excellence.

---

* John the Twenty-ſecond began his reign in 1316, died in 1334. Benedict the Twelfth was elected 1334, died 1342.

The

The Romans made this one of their ftations; from the deftruction of their empire to the fourteenth century, Avignon experienced numberlefs viciffitudes of fortune, and changes of mafters, in common with the reft of the country. In the year 1348 Joan queen of Naples, and countefs of Provence, being driven out of Italy, and unable to recover her Neapolitan crown through want of money, fold, or mortgaged this city to the Pope for eighty thoufand florins of gold, not thirty thoufand pounds fterling. The fovereign pontiffs fixed their feat here during a period of feventy-two years, and from hence ruled Europe with defpotic fway, though at the fame time they were mocked, and rejected by the factious people of Rome, and durft not truft their perfons within the walls of their own capital. Gregory the Eleventh, in 1377, yielded to the perfuafions of S. Catherina of Sienna, and the folicitations of the penitent Romans, and furmounting both his fear and refentment, eftablifhed once more the pontifical refidence at the Vatican. Since that time this territory has been governed by Legats, or Vicelegats. The Comtat Venaiffin had belonged to the Pope fince 1273, being a gift of Philip the Hardy, king of France.

The vices of an ecclefiaftical government, always fluctuating and ephemeral, operate even at this diftance to the difcouragement of induftry, trade, and population: the inhabitants fcattered over the face of one of the richeft plains in the univerfe, are not fufficiently numerous to cultivate it thoroughly; trade is not carried on with that emulation and activity, which ought to be infpired by the proximity of fo noble a river, and fo happy a fituation, in the center of a fertile country, and upon the great roads of communication between the Mediterranean and the capital of France. Smuggling indeed is purfued in a very fpirited manner with the adjacent provinces, but whether to the real advantage of the Comtat or not, is hard to determine: it either encourages idlenefs, or diverts the attention of the active part of the community from labours that would redound more to their own happinefs, and the welfare of the ftate. But can it be expected that an Italian prelate and his crew of fubaltern priefts, fhould feel themfelves fufficiently interefted in the profperity of a country, where their power is fhort lived, and which they always confider as foreign to them, to meditate, much lefs to execute projects for its amelioration?

Thefe

These and other reasons have led many speculators in politics to think, that the people of the Comtat would be great gainers, were the king of France to set aside the deed of sale by queen Joan, and incorporate it unalienably with the rest of his kingdom. I am clearly of another opinion; for what would the people gain? More neighbours to fill their plains and increase their culture—greater crowds on their roads, and clamour on their wharfs—more bustle in their streets, and more activity in their husbandry—some of their families would be illustrated by dignities and titles, and some enormous fortunes raised by trade, or the handling of the public revenue:—But with all these benefits, allowing them their highest value, must they not receive a swarm of devouring locusts, an army of tax-gatherers and monopolisers? Must not their taxes be prodigiously augmented, their salt, their tobacco, raised to such a price as to exclude the poorer class of citizens from a daily enjoyment of them? Must they not submit to the peremptory sway of intendants, subdelegates, military governors, and a long train of oppressive ministers, instead of the drowsy, but mild administration of their present masters, who want the power, if not the will, of raising more than the stipulated contributions? The inhabitants are too few for the extent of country, are indolent, and do not make the most of the riches nature presents on every side: I grant it, but they are already entitled to all the privileges of Frenchmen, if they choose to claim them, and at the same time they enjoy almost the independence of republicans. The first necessaries, and many of the superfluities of life, are cheap here; impositions are few and light; the husbandman is not dragged from his plough to garrison unwholesome fortresses, or pine in the cold and wet, to guard a coast against invaders: no districts are here reserved for the diversion of their sovereign, nor are their harvests devoured before their eyes by myriads of useless animals, which it is a capital offence to destroy, or even to molest. Then where shall I find a set of men that possess such means of happiness as the cultivators of this delicious plain?

L E T-

LETTER XXI.

Avignon.

HOW many times and how ardently have I not longed for a sight of Vauclufe; how many times have I not lamented that I had passed repeatedly through France, without extending my journey as far as the banks of the Sourgue, and the heavenly fields celebrated by Petrarch!

I have seen Vauclufe, and am disappointed. A huge cavern yawning at the foot of a perpendicular wall of bare rocks, and a large body of water issuing through the chinks of the stone, from an unfathomable pool that fills the cave, are undoubtedly bold, horrid features of nature; but I have seen the like in many mountainous countries in much greater perfection: here is not a single tree, not a bush to enliven the dull uniformity of the cliff, nor any lofty barrier of rock, over which the stream may rush in grand cascades; the landscape is dreary and frightful, without romantic beauty. From the ruins called Petrarch's Villa, the view extends over a fine country, but that immediately under the eye is not agreeable, though watered by the Sourgue meandering through the meadows. Vauclufe itself has not indeed answered my too sanguine expectations; but it is not so with the delightful vale I traversed before I reached this head of the Sourgue. A shady avenue of elms, poplars, and mulberry trees, led me insensibly from the gates of Avignon into the heart of a most fertile garden, for I can give no other name to a vast tract of level ground, where innumerable canals of the most limpid water impart a due degree of moisture to thousands of inclosures, covered with the greatest variety of productions; artificial and natural grasses, pulse, fruits, and corn are so intermingled, as to compose a lively many-coloured parterre: a chain of hills covered with vines, and crowned with tufts of trees, serve as the border to this rich expanse. I have also visited Orange, once the capital of a sovereign principality possessed by the families of Baux, Chalons, and last of Nassau: at present it is reunited to the royal domain. While France directed all its efforts towards the destruction of the Spanish power, the Stadtholders of Holland were maintained in their possession of this little state; but as soon as William the Third declared himself the opposer

J

and

and enemy of Lewis the Fourteenth, that monarch confifcated the principality of Orange ; each fubfequent peace ftipulated its reftitution ; but at laft, on the death of the king of England in 1702, Orange was declared to have efcheated to the crown of France. This forced fubmiffion, and the demolition of the proteftant churches, caufed a rapid emigration, and foon reduced the city to a ftate of poverty and folitude. Orange was a poft of confequence under the Romans, who called it Colonia Secundanorum, and erected many fumptuous edifices for the ufe and entertainment of its inhabitants: part of them are ftill to be feen. The principal monuments are, 1ft. A triumphal arch of the Corinthian order, now menacing ruin, the pillars that have been built to fupport it being too weak for the purpofe: it is decorated with trophies of various kinds, compofed of mafts, fails, and prows of gallies, fhields, coats of mail, helmets, and weapons: on the fhields are infcriptions not fatisfactorily decyphered by the learned. On one is MARIO, on another SACROVIR, a third has AVOD, and a fourth DACVDO, moft likely the names of foldiers or architects. The antiquarians of the country infift upon it that this monument was deftined to commemorate the fignal victory obtained by Caius Marius in the 61ft year of Rome, over the joint armies of the Cimbri and Teutones; they found their arguments upon the word Mario engraved on the fhield, and the head of a female figure reprefented looking out of a window, whom they take to be Martha the Syrian prophetefs, that accompanied Marius in his Gallic expedition : but there feems to be little reafon for a trophy being erected at Orange on account of a victory gained near Aix ; befides, the naval ornaments, and the tritons at the corners, point out a combat at fea, or upon the Rhone.—Other writers conjecture that it was raifed upon the defeat of the Allobroges, twenty years before. This arch is fixty feet in front, and profufely covered with fculpture, but the workmanfhip is not delicate, nor the defign agreeable ; the ftyle belongs to the age of Adrian and the Antonines. In that of Marius, and the conquerors of the Allobroges, architecture was in a rude ftate at Rome, and a monument erected by them would have been as plain and modeft as this is overcharged with ornaments and oftentatious. But Rome had not then deviated fo much from the auftere fimplicity of her republican principles, as to fuffer her generals to erect trophies of their victories. 2d. The ruins of a theatre vulgarly called *Le Cirque*. This building conveys a better idea of an antique theatre, and explains more clearly

its

its forms and diftribution than any remains now extant; for in all, except
thofe of the theatre at Tuormina, the *feena* is wanting. Here it is infinitely
more perfect than in Sicily, and confifts of two walls thirteen feet afunder; the
outermoft is of the ftupendous height of one hundred and fifteen feet, being
three hundred and thirty in length, covered in its whole extent by a broad
coping; the mafonry is regular, and unimpaired. Below the coping or cornice is a row of projecting ftones, bored through for the reception of tent
poles, to hold the awning over the fpectators. Next is a cordon, and at an
equal diftance beneath, another line of ftones that feem intended to fupport
the joifts of a floor: under them is a range of twenty-one falfe arches, the
center one of which exceeds the reft in height. Below is a third ftring of
toothings, and then, refting on the ground, an arcade of feventeen arches or
doors, at different intervals, and various elevations; the middle one is much
higher and wider than the others. Within this vaft line of building, a fecond
wall rifes to the height of the cornice, that covers the falfe arches; the middle
part of it is indented in a femicircular form, and was probably the *pulpitum*, or
part of the ftage principally devoted to the action, as two narrow fide doors
give admittance into it from the galleries, that filled up the fpace between the
walls. This interior wall is joined at each end to a large fquare tower
advancing into the *orcheftra* or pit, as far as the extremity of the benches, which
may yet be traced in a vaft femicircle on the declivity of the hill, to a height
equal with that of the front wall; they were all fo contrived as to afford the
fpectator a complete view of the ftage from every part of the femicircle.
The company entered by great gates on each fide between the benches and the
towers; the actors and workmen were admitted through the center door, which
anfwered to a hall under the ftage, and through four fmaller doors, that
opened into the lateral towers. The remaining twelve openings in the outer
wall ferved as entrances into magazines. This lofty pile croffes at right angles
a fmall oblong plain, even yet unincumbered with buildings; it has all the
appearance of having been the ftadium or field, where the Circenfian games
were exhibited; many parts of the wall, fuch as imperfect arches, interrupted
cornices, and toothings, indicate that there were galleries, and feats affixed to
it for the purpofe of beholding the races and other entertainments. The wall
thus ferved a double purpofe, and while it backed the *feena* of the theatre, was
employed alfo in fupporting feaffolds for the fhews of the Circus: it does not

I 2 feem

feem natural that this majeftic ruin fhould have acquired the uncommon name of a circus, had it never been any thing but a theatre, and therefore I am of opinion that the name has been handed down from the time of the Romans by a regular tradition.

The veftiges of an amphitheatre, part of an aqueduct, fome mofaics, and a few infcriptions, complete the lift of antiquities of Orange.

LETTER XXII.

Marfeilles, Nov. 14.

FROM Avignon we croffed a marfhy country and the river Dufance to St. Remy, a town built about a mile from the ruins of Glanum Livii. I was not able, during our fhort ftay, to difcover any other veftiges of the city than the two pieces of antiquity which had induced us to quit the poft road; one is a maufoleum, the other a triumphal arch; they ftand a few yards diftant from each other, but it does not appear to me that there ever was any connection between them, as is pretended by fome authors, who think that they were erected by the fame perfons, and in the Auguftan age. In my opinion they were built at very different periods of the art, the fculpture and architecture of the arch being much more chafte and perfect than thofe of the maufoleum; the latter is compofed of a pedeftal, ornamented in baffo relievo with combats of cavalry and infantry, over which hangs a net full of fifhes, and borne up by genii and mafks; at each angle is placed an Ionic pilafter; this pedeftal fuftains a fquare mafs, pierced through with an arch in each front, flanked by Corinthian columns; the architrave is charged with this infcription:

SEXLMIVLIEICFPARENTIBVSSVIS.

Sextus, Lucius, and Marcus, fons of Caius Julicius, *erected this* to their parents.

The frize is adorned with fnakes and winged dragons; above, is a circular pedeftal and colonnade of twelve fluted Corinthian pillars, fhort and thick in their proportions; the entablement is covered with a conical dome: under it appears a *togated* and a *ftolated* figure of very different ftature, without heads,

pro-

probably the effigies of the perfons to whofe memory this tomb was confecrated. The whole building is light and pleafing to the eye, but upon an examination of its feparate members, will be found faulty in many of its proportions; the columns are too fhort for their diameter, the roof is too heavy; perhaps, as was frequently the cuftom of the ancient mafters, the architect facrificed all confideration for the minuter parts to the general effect; and calculated the proportions fo as to produce a proper fenfation on the beholder at fome certain point of diftance, where the fituation of the ground, or the projection of adjacent buildings, obliged him to take his ftand to view it.

The arch has fuffered feverely by time and dilapidations; all the upper part is deftroyed, and only the gateway and a portion of the fide-walls fubfift. In both fronts the impofts, from which the arch fprings, reft upon pilafters, and on each fide of them are fluted columns of the Corinthian order, with their pedeftals, which fupported the general entablature, but fcarce a third of the fhafts remains. Between each pair of columns ftands the figure of a flave, one male, the other female, and in the triangle above the arch are the fragments of two winged victories: the ceiling of the gateway is delicately wrought in hexagon compartments. All that is yet left of this venerable pile befpeaks the happy tafte of architecture, that flourifhed under the firft Roman emperors; the fcience was then fimple and correct, not yet fophifticated by that furcharge of ornament which debafed and disfigured it in the following ages.

The country from hence grew bare and rocky; the banks of the rambling Durance ftony and difagreeable.

We paffed through Lambefe, a town belonging to the houfe of Lorraine; here the committee of the States of Provence is held: the ftates themfelves have not been called together fince the year 1639; but to fupply their place with greater convenience to government, the king iffues out a commiffion annually to the archbifhop of Aix, two bifhops, two gentlemen, the confuls of Aix, and thirty-five deputies of diftricts, ordering them to affemble under the direction of the military commandant, and the intendant of the province. In this meeting are fettled the free gifts to the king, and all extraordinary impofitions; the method of impofing and collecting the taxes is regulated by the number of families in each diftrict.

Aix,

Aix, the capital of Provence, and the feat of its parliament, lies in a bottom; the grounds that encircle it, are beautifully diverfified. Its fize is not confiderable, but the ftreets are of a convenient breadth, the fquares well planted, and the buildings folid; the town is plentifully fupplied with ftreams of water, flowing on all fides from the impending hills.

The Cours or Orbitelle is a magnificent walk above three hundred yards long, formed by a triple avenue of venerable elms, that fcreen two rows of regular and ftately houfes; it is refrefhed by four fountains; one of its extremities is clofed by the front of a church, the other admits a cheerful view of the country. The cathedral is a clumfy gothic pile; the cupola of its baptifmal font is fupported by fix columns of marble and two of granite, found among the ruins of a Roman palace. Here, and in the other churches of the city, are to be feen the tombs of feveral earls of Provence, and fome good pictures by French painters; in that of the Minims is a fmall elegant monument erected by Frederic the Second, king of Pruffia, to the memory of his friend the Marquis d' Argens, author of the *Lettres Juives.*

The civil buildings of this place are not remarkable, nor are there any great remains of antique magnificence, though this was the firft fettlement made in Gaul by the Romans : one hundred and twenty-four years before Chrift, C. Sextius Calvinius conducted an army hither, to fuccour the people of Marfeilles againft the Salvii, a Celtic tribe. The difcovery of fome tepid fprings determined the conful to fix a ftation in this valley, and thefe warm baths, which by habit, were become a neceffary part of the exiftence of a Roman, foon brought an affluence of inhabitants to the colony. The barbarian conquerors of Rome, who defpifed this luxury, overturned the fumptuous edifices that defended the waters and the bathers from injury, and buried the fprings under a mountain of ruins and rubbifh : it is not above a century fince they were accidentally brought again to light : they are fcarce warm, and almoft taftelefs, but are drunk in fpring by a concourfe of people, upon whom they operate as gentle deterfive phyfic.

A rocky road over parched-up waftes leads acrofs the hills towards Marfeilles. It is impoffible for either poet or painter to give an adequate idea of the wonderful view that burft at once upon us when we gained the fummit. The brown crag, that crowns the height where we ftood, flopes gently from it into thickets of evergreen flowering fhrubs: thefe cover a large circle below,

and

and terminate irregularly in fields of various culture, where the olive and other fruit trees are at first thinly dotted upon the grounds, but by degrees thicken into clumps, and foon into groves, till they form at laft one wide expanded foreft; beyond them, the apparent plain, for in reality it is a heap of little hills, is interfected in ten thoufand directions by walls, near each of which ftands a fmall pavilion called a baftide, as white as milk, ftrikingly oppofed to the greens and yellows of the gardens that furround it : a dark border inclofes this fpace, and feparates it from the fea, that immenfe body of waters which feems to be raifed half-way up to the firmament; the line of its horizon is loft at each extremity behind far diftant groupes of mountains; on its furface numberlefs fhips are fcattered like white fpots, changing their place with a motion not to be followed by the eye. In a femicircular bay, deeply cut into the fhore, lies the city of Marfeilles, huddled together, and defended by the iflands, that feem to block up the entrance of its narrow channel. I defcended with reluctance from this commanding ftation, and foon after beheld myfelf immured between high walls, fuffocated with duft, and poifoned by the ftench of the manure, which innumerable mules convey from the city to the vineyards.

LETTER XXIII.

Marfeilles.

WE have fettled ourfelves for a month in a villa without the gates;—and from our windows enjoy a profpect of great part of the city, bay, and iflands, with a fine ftretch of fea and coaft.

You who are acquainted with all my taftes and affections, may eafily conceive how my heart muft dilate, while I gaze upon fo admirable a picture in this cleareft of atmofpheres : you alfo well know with what enthufiafm I am fired when I read or talk of the exploits, the arts, the learning, and the virtues of ancient Greece ; and can therefore imagine with what veneration I view this Grecian colony, and meditate upon its hiftory, and that incomparable fyftem of adminiftration, which obtained the praife of the moft judicious authors among the ancients. Even now Marfeilles commands our

4

refpect

respect as a great commercial port; few cities can vie with it in extent of enterprize, in the various commodities displayed upon its wharfs, or in the number of veffels that fail from hence to all parts of the world; but thefe advantages are not entirely its own; it is now but an active member of a great monarchy, and I am confidering it, as it once was, miftrefs of itfelf, and the benefactrefs of. furrounding nations.

Six hundred years before Chrift, the inhabitants of the Ionian city of Phocea, having joined in the general but unfuccefsful infurrection of the Greek colonies in Leffer Afia, againft the Perfian king, fled to their fhips, and, rather than meet his vengeance, abandoned for ever the abode of their forefathers. They were long tofled about on the waves, and wandered to many ports in queft of a retreat, where they might enjoy the bleffings of liberty, and the fruits of their induftry : chance, or fome reafon unknown to us, brought them to the fhores of Gaul, where they built a city, called Maffylia. Their manners, inftitutes, and language continued for many ages to be Grecian ; their fame, as a trading nation, was equal to that of Carthage, and the fpirit, with which their navigators explored unknown coafts, was celebrated by the unanimous voice of antiquity. Their political inftitutes and internal adminiftration, were ftill more admired ; the wifdom, which directed their councils, preferved harmony at home, and eluded the malice, or repelled the infults of the neighbouring barbarians : but their fafety arofe from a fenfe of their favours, rather than the terror of their arms ; the Gauls were indebted to the Maffylians for inftruction of every kind ; the Maffylians were their mafters not only in morals, politics, and learning, but they alfo taught them how to procure the neceffaries and comforts of life with more eafe and certainty, and in greater abundance. Thefe benefits infured them the refpect and gratitude of the Gauls, till commerce, which feldom fails to corrupt the people it enriches, introduced vices that poifoned the fources from whence the profperity of the ftate had arifen. Then the Gauls began to perceive a change in the character of the Greeks, lefs probity in their dealings, and more ambition marked by the tranfactions of commerce; this gave birth to jealoufies, and no doubt provoked the Salvians to thofe hoftilities, which obliged the fenate of Marfeilles to call in the Romans, and thus afford that all-ufurping power a pretext for croffing the Alps. In the civil wars of Rome, Marfeilles took part with Pompey, was befieged, ftormed by Cæfar, and reduced to the ftate of a tributary.

In

In the decline of the Roman empire, Marseilles, having lost all virtue and energy with its independence, dwindled away to a mere ruin; nor did it recover any degree of consequence till one of the kings of Arles, in the ninth century, bestowed it as an appennage upon a younger son. It remained under the government of viscounts, or of its own magistrates, till the earls of Provence conquered it.

Marseilles stands upon a declivity and embraces the port, which runs about one thousand six hundred paces into the land. The old town is the most elevated, but it is ill built, filthy, and gloomy. The streets of the new town are spacious, and full of neat, good habitations. The Cours is a very noble street, planted with a double row of trees between lines of houses built upon a symmetrical design, and ornamented with porticos and columns. In the evening, especially that of a holiday, it is crowded with people, and forms one of the most variegated and lively scenes I ever beheld. This climate is excessively hot in summer, though tempered at certain hours by the breeze off the sea; in winter the north-east winds that blow for many weeks together, are the most cutting I ever felt; but when they cease, the winter days of this country are as pleasant as the finest summer ones in our northern regions.

In most of the churches are paintings of merit by Puget and other masters of the French school; but Puget's fame arises more deservedly from his admirable works in sculpture, of which many are to be seen in this his native city. The escutcheon of the royal arms over the door of the town hall, is a piece of exquisite taste and delicacy of touch.

The abbey of St. Victor contains a great quantity of tombs, and ancient inscriptions, in honour both of christians and pagans. It is one of the oldest monastical foundations in France; several eminent personages have belonged to its society, and there imbibed the principles of those virtues, and the rudiments of that knowledge, which afterwards raised them to the highest dignities of the church.

The harbour is shut up with a chain, and ships of war or heavy burden usually ride at anchor in the road between the islands and the main land, but there is always a great crowd of smaller vessels in the port; the usual number to be seen amounts at least to five hundred, and it is computed that near four thousand ships and barks enter this port in the course of a year. Along the

K

line

fine quay that lines it, the ftir and buftle is prodigious; a moving picture that is enlivened by the great variety of dreffes, the gefticulations and expreffive countenances of the perfons that compofe it.

The galley flaves, except when employed at work, chained in pairs, pafs their time in a part of the quay, lying near the gallies, which are ufed merely as places of confinement; this diftrict, I am told, is a kind of market for ftolen goods, as well as a receptacle of all forts of idle and profligate company. No place abounds more with diffolute perfons of both fexes than Marfeilles, and in the abundance of proftitutes, that appear in the ftreets, it is almoft upon a par with London.

The fortifications that defend the city on the land fide, are fuch as no military perfon would think able to refift the attacks of a regular army; and yet the emperor Charles the Fifth was foiled in his endeavours to break through them, and obliged to make a difgraceful retreat into Italy. Several forts guard the entrance of the harbour, and high upon the point of a mountain ftands that of Notre Dame de la Garde, better known by the mention made of it in the voyage of Chapelle and Bachaumont, than by its ftrength, or even its image of the Madonna, the patronefs of the Marfeillefe failors.

The Lazaretto is an extenfive infulated building. As the Levant trade, which is the great concern of Marfeilles, fubjects it to the dangers of the plague, and veffels are continually arriving from the fufpicious ports of Afia and Africa, the greateft care is neceffary to prevent this exterminating contagion from being communicated by any infected fhip. The laws of quarantine are no where better regulated, or more ftrictly enforced, than in this Lazaretto; nor is this to be wondered at, for the defolation of the year 1720 may be faid to be yet frefh in the memory of the inhabitants; fome furvivors remain to paint the horrid fcene, and keep alive the fears of thofe that are too young to have been witneffes of that dreadful vifitation of the hand of God. Above fixty thoufand perfons died of the diforder in the city of Marfeilles; but the lofs has been repaired, and it now reckons near ninety thoufand fouls within its walls. Of this multitude almoft every individual appears to have a concern in trade: I never faw a feaport, where there was fo much noife and buftle, but indeed I know no people of fo lively, clamorous a turn, or fo prone to boifterous joy, as that of Marfeilles. The Provençal is all alive, and feels his nerves agitated in a fupreme degree by

4   accidents

accidents and objects that would scarce move a muscle or a feature in the phlegmatic natives of more northern climes; his spirits are flurried by the slightest sensations of pleasure or of pain, and seem always on the watch to seize the transient impressions of either; but to balance this destructive propensity, nature has wisely rendered it difficult for those impressions to sink into their souls; they easily receive, but as easily discard and forget, thus daily offering a surface smoothed afresh for new pains and pleasures to trace their light affections upon. But this by no means excludes warm attachments and solid friendships; when time and habit afford leisure for the impression to penetrate deep enough, it will, no doubt, acquire and retain as firm a hold in their breast as in any other, and perhaps be stamped with still greater warmth and energy.

The commerce of Marseilles is divided into a multiplicity of branches; a variety of commodities are fabricated here, or brought from the other ports and inland provinces of France to be exported, and numerous articles of traffic are landed here in order to be dispersed in this and other kingdoms. It is presumed that one year with another business is transacted upon this exchange for near fifteen millions sterling. The exports to the Levant amount annually to thirty-one millions of livres; the imports from thence are valued at fifty. Those from the West Indies and Cayenne are calculated at seventeen millions of exports, and twenty-one of imports. About three millions and a half are employed in the East-India trade, six in the corn trade, and about twenty-nine in that with Spain and the rest of Europe. Four millions worth of salt cod and train oil comes from North America; oils from Sicily, &c. to the amount of fourteen millions, exported again in soap to nearly the same value; as also various manufactures to the amount of two millions and an half. Add to this circulation the dealings in insurances, and profits upon bullion, and you will have a rough, but comprehensive sketch of the commerce of Marseilles.

FINIS.

INDEX OF PLACES,

IN THE JOURNEY FROM

BAYONNE to MARSEILLES.

INDEX OF PERSONS,

IN THE JOURNEY FROM

BAYONNE TO MARSEILLES.

CONTENTS